Scholarship on Fire

A Personal Account of Fifty
Years of The Nazarene College
in Britain

Hugh Rae

First Fruits Press
Wilmore, Kentucky
c2017

Scholarship on fire: a personal account of fifty years of the Nazarene College in Britain.
By Hugh Rae.

First Fruits Press, © 2017

ISBN: 9781621717058 (print), 9781621717065 (digital), 9781621717072 (kindle)

Digital version at http://place.asburyseminary.edu/academicbooks/21/

First Fruits Press is a digital imprint of the Asbury Theological Seminary, B.L. Fisher Library. Asbury Theological Seminary is the legal owner of the material previously published by the Pentecostal Publishing Co. and reserves the right to release new editions of this material as well as new material produced by Asbury Theological Seminary. Its publications are available for noncommercial and educational uses, such as research, teaching and private study. First Fruits Press has licensed the digital version of this work under the Creative Commons Attribution Noncommercial 3.0 United States License. To view a copy of this license, visit http://creativecommons.org/licenses/by-nc/3.0/us/.

For all other uses, contact:

First Fruits Press
B.L. Fisher Library
Asbury Theological Seminary
204 N. Lexington Ave.
Wilmore, KY 40390
http://place.asburyseminary.edu/firstfruits

Rae, Hugh.
   Scholarship on fire: a personal account of fifty years of the Nazarene College in Britain / Hugh Rae. – Wilmore, KY: First Fruits Press, ©2017.
    192 pages: illustrations, portraits ; cm.
    Reprint. Previously published: Manchester, England: Agape, ©1994.
    ISBN: 9781621717058 (pbk.)
    1. Church of the Nazarene--England--Manchester--History. 2. Nazarene Theological College--History. 3. Theological seminaries--England--Manchester--History--20th century. I. Title.
BX8699.N32 R34 2017   207.42733

Cover design by Jon Ramsay

asburyseminary.edu
800.2ASBURY
204 North Lexington Avenue
Wilmore, Kentucky 40390

First Fruits Press
The Academic Open Press of Asbury Theological Seminary
204 N. Lexington Ave., Wilmore, KY 40390
859-858-2236
first.fruits@asburyseminary.edu
asbury.to/firstfruits

SCHOLARSHIP ON FIRE

A PERSONAL ACCOUNT OF FIFTY YEARS OF

THE NAZARENE COLLEGE IN BRITAIN

HUGH RAE

Agape Press Salford Manchester M6 6WL UK

Scholarship on Fire

Publisher:

Agape Press

An interdenominational resource centre for
***Advertising & Promotion, Design & Printing and
Distribution of Creative Christian Communication***

Agape Press, Unit 1D, Kingston Mill, Cobden Street, Salford, MANCHESTER M6 6WL. UK. Tel. 061-736 5496 Fax. 061-736 5497

CONTENTS

	Page
PREFACE	3
FOREWORD	5
Chapter 1	8
THE PREPARED SOIL	
Chapter 2	18
A MAN OF VISION	
Chapter 3	30
THE STRUGGLE TO SURVIVE	
Chapter 4	38
MUCH ADO ABOUT NOTHING	
Chapter 5	49
CHANGE IN LEADERSHIP	
Chapter 6	60
BEECH LAWN BIBLE COLLEGE	
Chapter 7	68
THE DILEMMA OF LOCATION	
(Uniting Two Colleges)	
Chapter 8	75
NEW DIRECTION NEW CHALLENGE	
Chapter 9	88
A NEW HAND AT THE HELM	
Chapter 10	103
WHEN ENOUGH IS NOT ALLOWED TO BE ENOUGH	
Chapter 11	111
VISION AND ITS COST	
Chapter 12	125
A VISION REALISED	
Chapter 13	138
DEVELOPING A TEAM	
Chapter 14	150
LIFE DOES NOT STAND STILL	
Epilogue	158
Appendix 1	165
The Quest for British Degree Validation Kent E Brower	
Appendix 2	179
GOVERNORS	
Appendix 3	181
CITATION OF MERIT	
REFERENCES	182
INDEX OF PHOTOGRAPHS	183

DEDICATION

To the memory of
Revd Dr George Frame

PREFACE

My purpose is to give the reader information and insight into the work and life of Nazarene Theological College, Manchester. In recording the developments of campus, student life, and curriculum it is my intention to give a sense of the excitement which the changes have produced over these fifty years.

This is not an exhaustive history of the college but is much more a personal recollection of events and people over this fifty year period. The mistakes are all mine, the perception and evaluations are those of the author alone. It has been the intention to give an honest summary of these years. Many people have helped me in the final drafting of the manuscript and I would be remiss if I failed to mention some of these.

Dr Tom Noble has readily advised me at several points and given valuable guidance. Dr Kent Brower has supplied excellent information for the chapter which deals with the granting of degree status through CNAA. I have included the full text which he kindly drafted in Appendix 1.

Dr Herbert McGonigle, the present Principal of the college, has read the manuscript and readily written the Foreword to the book. Revd Gordon Thomas, Dean of Students, read sections of the manuscript and made valuable suggestions. A draft of earlier chapters was read by my longtime friend and colleague, Revd Dr Sydney Martin, who with many others helped make this history possible. My wife Nan read and corrected early proofs and patiently allowed me all the time I needed to write.

Our two children, Peter Rae and Marjory Szurko, have read through the manuscript and made editorial and other helpful suggestions which have gone to greatly improve the structure of this history.

My sincere thanks and appreciation must go to my publisher Dr. D. E. Okpalugo of Agape Press, for his patient guidance in getting this manuscript to press. His commitment to the project has been exceptional as has his christian witness at all times.

To each of these I give my sincere thanks and know that the finished book has been greatly improved by their help.

To the readers I can only hope that you find enjoyment as well as information in reading the book. Its title was suggested by Dr McGonigle and reflects the memory of the founding Principal, Dr George Frame, and his early hope that the college would indeed become an academic institution of note and that always at its heart the warmth of commitment to the message of Full Salvation would burn. There are many interesting events left out and it may be that some whose lives were touched by the college will feel that these should have been included. I can only hope that you will understand how difficult it has been to decide what to use and what to leave unwritten.

In dedicating this book I am conscious of the part played by many people over these fifty years. My wife and family, my colleagues for whom I have the highest regard, college governors who trusted me and gave me such support over the years and last but by no means least a great host of students who through the years have added such joy to our lives. To all I offer this book as a tribute to the love and faithfulness which each has exemplified. My prayer is that Nazarene Theological College will remain true to its purpose and influential in its ministry.

FOREWORD

This year 1994 is the Golden Jubilee year of the Nazarene Theological College in Manchester. It is a most appropriate year in which to publish the college's history and it is equally appropriate that Dr Hugh Rae should write that history. No one has had a longer or a closer acquaintance with the college than Dr Rae. Just as St. Luke prefaces his Gospel by saying that he had had full knowledge of these things from the beginning, Dr Rae could well have claimed likewise for this story. And what a story it is, taking us from the inauspicious beginnings of a small Bible training college near Glasgow in 1944 to a theological college in Manchester in 1994 which offers students many qualifications, ranging from a one-year certificate to a PhD in affiliation with Manchester University.

Dr Rae has recaptured well the uncertainties and hesitations of many of the 1000 Nazarenes in Britain in 1944 when Dr George Frame challenged them to open their own theological college. After all, it was war time, resources of all kinds, including potential students, were scarce and buying property and hoping to find both suitable staff and students seemed a risky enterprise. But Dr Frame had courage as well as vision and against all the odds, Hurlet Nazarene College was opened near Paisley, Scotland, in September 1944. Although there were only two full-time students in that first term, Dr Frame's vision was for a Holiness college that would combine the best of academic endeavour and spiritual fervour and so the college's motto was born, "Scholarship On Fire."

It was a further wise move made by Dr Frame that appointed Revd Hugh Rae as college Dean in 1952 and Principal from 1954. For a total of 27 years, stretching from 1952 to 1986, (with a break between 1966 and 1973) the influence of Dr and Mrs Hugh Rae on the consolidation and development of the college is incalculable. They brought skill, dedication and sacrifice to the task and the Nazarene College owes more to them than can be expressed. In particular, the foundations for the college's recently-acquired affiliation with Manchester University and its almost doubling of student numbers were laid by Dr Rae's far-sighted leadership when he returned for his second term as Principal in 1973.

In this history Dr Rae writes carefully, comprehensively and perceptively of the college's fifty years. It is a story told, in Cromwell's famous phrase, "warts and all." Here are the hallelujahs and the heartbreaks, the crowns and the crosses, the pleasure and the pain that reflect the reality of Christ's kingdom on earth. It is not always victory all the way in everything when working with the people of God, even the best of God's people. This history of the Nazarene College is all the more valuable because it is realistic and Dr Rae has written fairly and openly of the men and women whom we meet in its pages.

The author has also achieved something else. He has written objectively of a history in which he himself was so much involved for so long. With his characteristic modesty, his own vital contribution to the college's development over many years receives little attention in these pages. Hopefully this Foreword will go some way to remedy that omission. One other observation needs to be made. We all read history with our own hermeneutic and thereby come to our own conclusions. Dr Rae has wisely subtitled his work "A Personal Account." This does not detract from the objectivity of the history but it does allow the author to state his convictions and conclusions about events and people where others may think somewhat differently.

Having the honour to succeed Dr George Frame, Dr Jack Ford and Dr Hugh Rae as Principal of the (now) Nazarene Theological College, I warmly commend Dr Rae's history to all our people and to all others who will read it. It is carefully researched and well written and is a most fitting publication for our Jubilee year. On behalf of my colleagues on the staff, I pledge our endeavours, under God and with His grace, to continue what Dr Rae and his predecessors worked and planned and prayed and sacrificed for - that the Nazarene College might always embody Scholarship on Fire.

Herbert McGonigle
N T C   *June 1994*

Photo No 1
Revd Dr George Sharpe founder of Pentecostal Church of Scotland

Chapter 1

THE PREPARED SOIL

The community was buzzing with the news that Revd George Sharpe had been evicted from the pulpit of the Parkhead Congregational Church in Glasgow on Saturday evening, 29th September, 1906, and that more than 80 people wanted him to continue as their minister. The following day, Sunday, September 30th, they met in the Great Eastern Road Halls and a new church was born. Sharpe himself, born and brought up in Motherwell, had been a Methodist minister in New York State. He had already proved his preaching and administrative ability and on October 17th "Parkhead Pentecostal Church" was organised with four of the former deacons of the Congregational Church serving as deacons for the new congregation.

The division in Parkhead Congregational Church came about because George Sharpe was a passionate advocate of Christian holiness as taught by John Wesley, the founder of Methodism, and proclaimed by the nineteenth century Holiness Movement. The main emphasis of the Holiness people was that entire sanctification was a definite second work of grace entered into by faith subsequent to regeneration.

The Wesleyan emphasis on Christian holiness was widely influential at this time in Evangelical churches on both sides of the Atlantic. In Britain, William Booth (a Methodist preacher) launched the Salvation Army in 1865. In 1886 John George Govan founded the Faith Mission, working mainly in the Scottish Highlands and Ireland. The Pentecostal League of Prayer, formed in 1891 by Reader Harris, Q.C., had its headquarters at Speke Hall in Battersea, and was led, after Harris' death, by Oswald Chambers.

In the same year that George Sharpe founded his new church in Glasgow, the businessman David Thomas, one of Reader

Harris's lieutenants, was questioning the strategy of his spiritual father and mentor - that the way to influence the church in general towards the message of heart holiness was to form an interdenominational league of people remaining in their established churches. Instead, Thomas gathered a group of his own employees around him and began the work which became the International Holiness Mission. Another centre for the same purpose was Star Hall in Manchester, founded as an independent mission by Francis Crossley, a prosperous business man.

Within Methodism itself, Thomas Champness had begun the Joyful News Mission which was to lead, in 1904, to the founding of Cliff College under Thomas Cook. Earlier, the Keswick Convention was established in 1874. Its emphasis on Christian holiness, while departing from classical Wesleyan doctrine, was to have wide interdenominational influence.

It was not the intention of George Sharpe to found a new denomination, but events rapidly made such a proposition inevitable. From his centre at Parkhead in Glasgow, churches sprang up in Paisley, Uddingston, Motherwell and Edinburgh. Independent missions in Perth and Blantyre wanted to associate with him. The result was the formation of the Pentecostal Church of Scotland in 1909. The label "Pentecostal," widely used in the Wesleyan Holiness Movement, was later dropped because it became associated with speaking in tongues.

There now developed a very real need for pastoral leadership. Most of the initial leadership was carried out by laymen, but for the church to grow, Sharpe believed it would be necessary to find men with the gifts required. That would mean that they would need theological education, which in turn meant thinking about a theological college. This would not be an easy task for the fledgling denomination. Resources were very limited, but the need for such a venture soon became imperative. The question then was not whether a training college was needed but rather where and how one could be established.

Dr Jack Ford comments on this early attempt to establish a Bible school:

On September 22nd, 1908, Sharpe inaugurated the Parkhead Holiness Bible School, declaring that such a school had been laid on his heart ever since the opening of the church. He defined its purpose as twofold: firstly, the training of young men and women "in all the fullness of the Gospel" in order that they might preach "an uttermost salvation for all in this and other lands"; and, secondly, as a help to those who, "though not specially called to preach", desired to know more of the "wonderful truth of Entire Sanctification." The course included Theology, Homiletics, New Testament, Work and Methods, Grammar and English Composition.[1]

Thus within two years of the Parkhead Pentecostal Church being founded, a Bible college was in existence to train men and women for ministry. The fact that Sharpe founded this Bible school in September 1908, prior to other local congregations asking to join him, would suggest that he was already anticipating growth further afield than Parkhead and wanted to be prepared for it.

It is clear that Sharpe was following the pattern set by the Holiness Movement in the United States, where it was recognised that an educated ministry was essential if growth and consolidation were to take place. Ford reminds us, when speaking about this Bible school that:

This venture was taken up with enthusiasm. In the region of forty or fifty students enrolled, and between twenty and thirty completed the first year's course (according to the Bible College minutes.) The teachers were Mr and Mrs Sharpe, their eldest daughter Katherina Elizabeth, and Mr Joseph Robertson, the Secretary of the Pentecostal League of Prayer at Motherwell ... from among the students in those early classes arose some of the first ministers of the Pentecostal Church of Scotland: notably, Andrew Robertson, the secretary and treasurer of the school, John E. Watson, Peter Clark and Robert Purvis.[2]

An advertisement in *The Way of Holiness,* published in 1909 by Star Hall, the Holiness centre in Manchester, gives a listing of the offerings at this Holiness Bible college, which met in Parkhead Pentecostal Church, Glasgow. Three courses were available:

Evangelists' Course	- Two Years
Licentiates' Course	- Two Years
Ministerial Course	- Four Years

A correspondence course was also offered through Miss Olive Winchester, A.B., a graduate of Harvard who was preparing to graduate as the first woman to receive a BD degree from the University of Glasgow. This advertisement suggests an ambitious training programme. It is evident that the Holiness people in Britain were conscious of the fact that an educated leadership was essential. The problem, however, was one of finance. How could one expect a few hundred people, however enthusiastic, to finance and maintain an educational establishment of even minimal size?

The teaching staff were all part-time but when, in due course, property was purchased the demand on resources was considerable. This property, at 1 Westbourne Terrace, Kelvinside, Glasgow, was a spacious terrace house in the West End of the city. It had three floors, with large, commodious rooms which housed the Sharpe family and other visitors, as well as providing housing for the small band of students.

Ford says:

From the inception of the denomination, the idea of a separate college building persisted, especially in Sharpe's mind. By the close of 1912, on his return from America, where he had received gifts for this purpose, he secured a suitable building on his own initiative, deferring, however, to the authority of the Educational Committee by asking them to name it. They approved its legitimacy by christening it, "The Pentecostal Bible College" (one of the names submitted by its father!) The Fifth Assembly was informed that it was Sharpe's intention that they should adopt it, as soon as it was finished and occupied. It cost £800, a princely sum in 1912.

On August 16th, 1913, it was officially opened by Dr A. M. Hills, and the following September the 1913-14 session commenced there with "three resident students, three visiting students and one correspondence student." It was a big undertaking for such a small denomination. Miss Winchester returned to America in June 1914. The country was on the eve of a war which would draw all available young men into the forces or the factories.

Sharpe withstood the inevitable to the end, faithfully tutoring his last student until his call-up in June 1916. He was the chief mourner at the funeral of his untimely child.[3]

There were those who criticised the whole financial undertaking. There is no doubt that it was a real venture of faith on Sharpe's part, not unlike that to be followed by one of his successors three decades later. The Great War of 1914-18 was the final blow to an already struggling effort. The vision, however, was alive, even though the infant denomination was not as yet able to financially sustain the college.

It is of historical interest that at this same time Star Hall had also begun a Bible Training School for women. Associated with the early days of this venture was A. M. Hills, DD, a man of considerable influence in the early years of the Church of the Nazarene. His *Systematic Theology*, published in 1931, was to become the standard text until the publishing of Orton Wiley's three volumes in 1940. Hills was to be the first President of the Illinois Holiness University, later to become Olivet Nazarene College and University.

Photo No 2
1 Westbourne Terrace, Kelvingrove, Glasgow

During these years the leaders of the Pentecostal Church of Scotland began to talk about union with the rapidly growing Holiness body in the United States of America which itself had come into being as a result of several unions, the most important being that which had taken place at Pilot Point Texas in 1908.

At Chicago in 1907 a union had taken place between the Church of the Nazarene, based in Los Angeles, led by Phineas F. Bresee and the Association of Pentecostal Churches of America, based in New York, led by Hiram F. Reynolds. Then in 1908, at Texas, the Holiness Church of Christ united with the Pentecostal Church of the Nazarene, whose name was retained. Olive Winchester seemed to be the catalyst in bringing Dr E. F. Walker, a General Superintendent in the Pentecostal Church of the Nazarene, to Scotland where he met with Sharpe and others. After lengthy negotiations and by a large majority vote of the churches, the Pentecostal Church of Scotland merged with the Pentecostal Church of the Nazarene in November 1915. "Pentecostal" was dropped from the title four years later.

The British churches (including Morley and Gildersome in Yorkshire) became the British Isles "District" of the Church of the Nazarene and George Sharpe was appointed District Superintendent. Now, as the end of the First World War neared, he was in need of trained preachers if the work of the new denomination was to move ahead. With the closing of the college in 1916 the question of men for ministry was a pressing one, and so the home study course provided for in the *Manual* of the Pentecostal Church of the Nazarene was introduced.

One of the new recruits to the ministry in the ten years after union, J. D. Lewis, had trained with the Faith Mission College in Edinburgh. Others came from a variety of denominational backgrounds but came to evangelical faith in their teens in the Church of the Nazarene. This period produced men like Kenneth McRitchie, George Frame, James B. Maclagan and James Macleod, each of whom has a unique place in the annals of the British Church of the Nazarene. Many others fell by the wayside and it may well be that the struggle to complete a course of study for ordination, complicated by earlier loyalties, made it difficult to maintain long term ministry. If the Church of the Nazarene in Britain was to establish itself on a firm foundation and be seen as a growing movement it would need to find some way of training its own young people for ministry.

A further attempt was made to establish a college in Scotland:

The Board of Education urged the 1926 Assembly to commence a Bible school. The recommendation was adopted and

George Sharpe undertook the task of establishing a British Nazarene College in Motherwell. But shortage of students, lack of support from the district and sickness in his family conspired against the new venture. The college was opened in October, 1926, and closed in June, 1928.[4]

The growth of the church during its first two decades had been slower than anticipated. Though the need for a college was always seen as important to such growth, the climate was still not ripe. The world was moving into what was to be the great depression, and even some of the church's American colleges, established on a much firmer financial base than was feasible in Britain, were to face such pressures that they closed their doors for a time.

This made the second attempt, spearheaded by Sharpe, an unlikely candidate for success. Its closure, though unwelcome, was not unexpected. It was undoubtedly a bitter disappointment to Sharpe. Two of the students enrolled at this time were Murdoch Luke, stepbrother of Robert Purvis, and David Anderson. Murdoch Luke became the first pastor at the new church in Troon, but he was to move to the United Free Church of Scotland. David Anderson was to become an esteemed and much loved pastor until his untimely death in 1954. When Robert Purvis, one of the two graduates of Sharpe's first college, became District Superintendent in 1930, the continual calls for a college still went unanswered, for although the church saw new growth, the depression years made funding a college impossible.

Throughout these years various classes met and courses were taught. In Gallowgate, near Parkhead Cross, the Messenger Publishing Company, managed by Dr Sharpe, was used as the venue where pastors-in-training took classes under the direction of the District Board of Examiners. Though the programme lacked cohesion and structure, it did ease some of the burden of preparation and gave at least minimal guidance to the students.

The Church of the Nazarene in Britain, then, was constantly concerned about the education of its ministry, although meagre resources placed a retarding hand on the possible development of a college. The General Assembly of the international church tried to include Britain within the zone of Canadian Nazarene College, then located at Red Deer, Alberta, but this proved impractical. The cost of travel and fees made it difficult for the British church to use the facilities. When one student, William Clark, did go there in the late 1930s the cultural differences and lifestyle seemed to unsettle him. He returned to pastor the church in Belfast but after a brief ministry he went to another denomination.

The establishment of a college had twice been frustrated and the work of education was left to other colleges, such as the Faith Mission College in Edinburgh and Emmanuel College in Birkenhead, England.

By 1940 members of the District Council of the Nazarene Young People's Society were pressing the District Assemblies to found a college. Their urgent proposals were an indication that people were becoming conscious of the fact that the growth of the denomination made such a proposition both desirable and viable. The climate was changing, and it was no longer only the leadership which was aware of the need. Young laymen were realising that this project was essential and with that realisation went an awareness of the responsibility which such an event would bring.

The beginning of the Second World War was to set back for a time the possibility of founding a college. Men and women were being conscripted into the armed forces and drafted into all kinds of war work. The possibility of getting students to enrol under such circumstances was slight. It was therefore a very real challenge of faith to purchase West Hurlet House, Nitshill, Glasgow in the autumn of 1943.

Photo No 3
Revd Dr George Frame, Founding Principal of
Hurlet Nazarene College, Barrhead, Glasgow

Chapter 2

A MAN OF VISION

Only a fool - or a man of extraordinary faith and vision - would try to establish a theological college in the middle of a world war. The late Dr George Frame was no fool. In 1943 the outcome of the Second World War was far from certain, yet it was in this climate that Hurlet Nazarene College was founded.

There can be little dispute over the fact that Hurlet Nazarene College owed a great debt to the insight, foresight and personality of George and Emily Frame. They were a remarkable couple and their sacrificial commitment to the infant college underlined their courage and insight.

George Frame had been converted in his late teens under the anointed ministry of Revd James Jack in the Parkhead Church of the Nazarene. Sensing the call of God, George Frame responded and began to prepare himself for the Christian ministry. Though in many respects a shy, retiring man, as the years passed he revealed a commitment to the church and an administrative ability that was to take him in 1940 into the superintendency, where he served for thirty-two years.

George Frame and James Baxter Maclagan were colleagues and, in some ways, competitors. Both had prepared for the ministry through the home study course. Classes were given on an *ad hoc* basis but these were very limited in scope, leaving the students to do most of their own reading and preparation for examinations. The value of such class work was appreciated by these pastors although they were also aware of the limitations of such a method of study. Although "J. B.", as he was affectionately called, did not have the opportunity to do formal academic work, he nevertheless constantly encouraged other young men to get the best preparation possible. He knew the value of college training and was a supporter of any decision which would make such training possible.

In the 1930s Frame was pastoring the Church of the Nazarene in Uddingston, near Glasgow, and it was while there that he attended the University of Glasgow, graduating with the MA degree. He and Revd James Macleod (who prior to entering the ministry had graduated with a BSc) were the only two ordained elders to have completed academic work at a university. One might have expected that Frame would be anxious for others to follow in his footsteps, but he often seemed to discourage men from following along the path. Perhaps he was afraid that some good men would be lost to the Liberalism of the divinity halls of the forties. Or was he living up to his reputation of being a veritable bundle of contradictions?

When Robert Purvis became District Superintendent in 1930 the membership of the church was 744 and this increased to 1001 by 1940. The number of churches in 1931 was 16. Two of these, Morley and Gildersome, were in England. By 1940, when Purvis resigned, there were 25 churches, a very small number of congregations to be asked to support a college. Apart from Parkhead and Morley all the congregations were under 100 members and most were less than 30 members. There was considerable pressure on the delegates at several District Assemblies in the late 1930s to establish a training college for men and women entering the ministry. It seemed, however, that this would not happen for many years. Young men like Joseph Irvine, Thomas Wilson, and William Taylor were preparing themselves theologically through the home study course. Others, like William Clark and Jack MacDonald, crossed the Atlantic, enrolling at Canadian Nazarene College, Alberta, and Pasadena College, California, respectively. This method was not a viable proposition and only served to highlight the need for a British college.

These developments, and the growing need for pastors, convinced Frame that steps must be taken to remedy the situation. In many cases pastors had been recruited from other groups, but there were many serious losses, and many who came did not remain long with the church. These facts meant that real growth and development was more likely to come with the establishing of a theological college.

From the outset Frame was insistent that this should be a theological college, not simply a Bible training college. His philosophy at that point was not always appreciated but he knew that the distinction was important. His choice of a motto for the college clearly reveals his twin desire for evangelism to go hand in hand with scholarship: "Scholarship on Fire." He could not envisage the one without the other nor did he reckon them incompatible. In 1940, when Frame became District Superintendent, Europe was already embroiled in the Second World War: the prospects for peace seemed far away. In these circumstances, with the British wing of Church of the Nazarene effectively cut off from the United States, there was much uncertainty as to the future.

During the early 1940s George Frame's term of office in the superintendency was somewhat in doubt. His leadership and personality were very different from those of his predecessor, Robert Purvis. In some ways he appeared to be unemotional whereas Purvis had seemed warm-hearted. In addition, Frame and Maclagan had often challenged the leadership of Purvis at District Assemblies, and been rivals for the leadership role. Many had not viewed the change with favour and blamed them for the resignation of Purvis. However, by 1943, matters had stabilised somewhat and the church was holding its own despite the fact that many of its young people were serving in the forces. Nevertheless the wholehearted support which the founding of a college would need from the District was not at this stage forthcoming.

It was in the midst of this uncertainty that the District Advisory Board, accepting the insight of Frame (and because of the constant pressure by the young people at every District Assembly since 1938) began to consider seriously the purchasing of property designed to serve as a college. The property known as West Hurlet House was the place chosen, and, after much prayer, the decision was finally made to purchase this Georgian mansion, which stood in some ten acres of land on the boundary between the city of Glasgow and the town of Barrhead.

Photo No 4
West Hurlet House, Barrhead, Glasgow

The grey sandstone building had three storeys. Built towards the end of the reign of George IV, about 1830, it had a two-storey annexe, which had served as servant accommodation. There were in addition two smaller houses which could serve as staff housing when required. The price paid for the property was £4000. Since the average wage for a working man in 1943 was about £5 per week, this was a giant step of faith. In 1943 there were 925 church members to bear this cost.

No sooner was West Hurlet purchased than there were those who spoke of the deal as a foolhardy venture. Some referred to the building as a "White Elephant", owing to some serious problems with dry rot. Others were of the opinion that since men and women were still in the forces this was a bad time to buy, while yet others were sceptical about the ability of the church to finance such a venture.

With the purchase of the property it was imperative to get a programme launched as quickly as possible... but how? The sudden deaths in 1938 of William Taylor, then pastor of Morley, and in 1943 of Joseph Irvine, perhaps the most promising of the younger pastors, meant that some who might well have taken over college leadership were gone.

In 1941 the Uddingston church had called Revd Arthur Fawcett to be their pastor. He had been the founding pastor of the International Holiness Mission church at Bolton. His coming as Frame's successor at Uddingston was seen as an important move. Fawcett had been a student at Cliff College, was a powerful preacher and an excellent pastor. Soon after coming to Uddingston he followed the example set by Frame and enrolled at the University of Glasgow. After taking an Honours MA in History he proceeded to take his BD degree at Trinity College, Glasgow. He had the undoubted qualifications and potential to be the Principal of the new college.

However, he and George Frame were not always in agreement as to policy and, in addition, he was seen by some as an outsider who might not uphold the "Nazarene" traditions. There were some occasions when the conflict between Frame and Fawcett spilled over in public. We will never know what might have been the development of Hurlet had Fawcett been invited to become Principal. By 1950 he was working on a doctoral thesis, which saw him resign his pastorate in Uddingston and ultimately enter the ministry of the Church of Scotland. All of this meant that the sources of potential leadership were small and the future of the new college was placed in some jeopardy. The initial development of the work of the college was to be left in other hands.

Photo No 5
George and Emily Frame with son Cyril

George Frame and his family took up residence at Hurlet Nazarene College (as the college was named) in the latter part of 1943. Their home in Uddingston was given up and they paid rent at Hurlet, which helped with the running costs. George Frame assumed the responsibilities of Principal, though he drew salary only for his role as District Superintendent.

By September, 1944, the first classes were meeting. Most of the potential young people were either in the armed forces or involved in war work. Thus the first class had only two full-time students, Arthur Smith and Leslie Newton, both from Morley, near Leeds. In addition, some pastors on the home study course were required to attend lectures. These included Ernest Eades and William Russell (both graduates of Emmanuel College, Birkenhead), and Sydney Martin. Betty Edgington from South Shields joined the student body in September, 1945. This inauspicious beginning caused some to feel that this too might fail and to fear serious monetary loss to the struggling church in Britain.

Then in April, 1945, the war with Germany was over. Arthur Smith had dropped out of college, but Alfred S. Milliken and Hugh Rae, both from the church in Troon, joined the remaining two full-time students. Would this change in the world situation mean that the college would survive? The real issue was still financial. In 1945 George Frame, Arthur Fawcett and James Macleod were joined by other pastor-tutors such as Dr George Sharpe (then in his eighties), J. D. Lewis, William Robertson and David Anderson. The curriculum was designed to cover the essential course for ordination. Of course, the level of teaching varied in accordance with the educational and teaching ability of the men. They all gave of their best, but some, like Fawcett and Frame, proved more successful in stimulating their students to learn. There is no doubt that these were difficult days, but George Frame pursued his ideal with courage and vigour.

Filling the dual roles of District Superintendent and college Principal was no easy task, and in consequence some essential development in both areas was postponed for several years. A returning serviceman, John Walker, was engaged as Warden. His responsibilities were never clearly defined and the resulting frustration saw him and his wife resign only a few months after taking up residence. He was replaced by a couple from Ilkeston, Mr and Mrs John Mitchell. The question of discipline and authority was never clearly established and they soon resigned from the post. For a brief time Revd David Anderson took over the role, but his time was divided between the college and publishing interests. Revd Peter Clark assumed the responsibility as Dean of Students and Business Manager from 1948 until his retirement in 1952.

In September, 1946, the student body increased from four to ten. Three of the new students were from Ireland: George Stewart, Robert Noble, Alan Loney. Three were from England: James Humphries, James Osman, and George James Green. These numbers were added to by visiting pastors, who were completing their studies. The most outstanding of these was Sydney Martin, who, immediately upon ordination, was to return as a part-time instructor in Church History. This was the beginning of the slow climb to an enrolment of twenty students, which was to remain the top number until the seventies.

The need for a full-time Principal was evident but George Frame seemed unable or unwilling to relinquish the leadership during this formative period. The minutes of the Board of Trustees reveal that year after year the matter of a Principal was raised. Perhaps if Frame had resigned as District Superintendent, he could have given his full attention to the college. The fact is that there were rumblings of discontent and in the District Assembly of 1948 he was not re-elected on the first ballot. Perhaps he should have taken that as a guide. In the event, when others withdrew their names he was re-elected and was to serve until 1972.

At a meeting of the Board of Trustees held on 27th May, 1946 the following minute was recorded: "The matter [of a Principal] was discussed at some length and then it was decided to write to Revd S. T. Ludwig, General Secretary of the Church of the Nazarene, in Kansas City, for information concerning any possible candidate."5

The college seemed destined to struggle for a longer period without a full-time Principal. Potentially promising students like Jim Osman, who were dissatisfied with this state of affairs, withdrew from the college and were lost to full-time ministry. Such men were a loss to the church at large and were perhaps part of the price paid for the failure to meet the need for a full-time Principal.

That does not mean that Frame would not have been prepared to see such an appointment made, but he seemed to feel that the time was not ripe and he, more than any other, had a deep desire to see this college firmly established.

At an undated meeting of the trustees, prior to 16th August 1947, *Dr George Sharpe stated,*

...that in his opinion someone with academic qualifications was required and that Brother Frame should consider it. There was further discussion over the question of a dual role after which Dr Sharpe moved that Mr Frame be recognised as Principal, and we accept any arrangement Mr Frame might make regarding a deputy⁶.

On 16th August, 1947, *Mr Frame said that the increased number of students now required that a full-time Principal be appointed.*⁷

In 1947, while these discussions were taking place, the leaders of the Calvary Holiness Church entered into discussion with the leaders of the Church of the Nazarene in Britain. The Calvary Holiness Church was a group which had separated from the International Holiness Mission under the leadership of Revd Maynard James. The idea was mooted that both denominations share in the running of a Holiness college in Britain for the training of ministers, to ease the financial burden for both groups. The proposal was overtaken by events when the General Church of the Nazarene recognised Hurlet as a denominational College of Higher Education and thereafter gave a measure of financial support. The Calvary Holiness Church then purchased Beech Lawn at Uppermill, Cheshire, in 1947, and founded what was to become Beech Lawn Bible College. The two colleges were to come together in 1955 when Union took place between the Calvary Holiness Church and the Church of the Nazarene.

In 1949 the General Nazarene Young People's Society in America, Canada and Britain raised $10,000 for Hurlet in order to clear the capital indebtedness. A subsequent devaluation of the pound sterling meant that the $10,000 (when exchanged to pounds) produced enough surplus cash to clear a large repair account which had occurred as a result of the dry rot problem, so by 1950 the property was free of debt.

In 1950, six years after the first classes met, the college still did not have a full-time teacher let alone a resident staff. That year, Frame invited Joseph Kenneth Grider to come and live at the college, give some oversight and teach, while pursuing his doctoral studies at the University of Glasgow. Grider had graduated from Olivet Nazarene College and Nazarene Theological Seminary in Kansas City. He and his wife, Virginia, consented to come for two years and lived in the college. He taught theology while his wife assisted in several areas of college life. Grider's coming to the college added fresh life and gave promise of other such men coming to assist in the days ahead.

Photo No 6
Students and Staff at front entrance of Hurlet in 1948

In some ways Grider was to George Frame what Olive Winchester had been to George Sharpe three decades earlier. She had come to study at the University and taught classes in the first residential college which had closed in 1916. Now George Frame was being ably assisted in the classroom by one who was later to make a great contribution to the church as Professor of Theology at the Seminary. But this was still only a stopgap, since Grider had no intention of being a permanent member of the staff at Hurlet.

In 1952, the Griders returned with their baby daughter to the United States and Frame began, during the 1952 General Assembly in Kansas City, to interview couples who might follow the Griders' example and come to teach while studying. The result of those interviews forms another chapter in the life of the college, one which was to have long-term implications for the infant institution.

That same year negotiations took place which resulted in the union between the International Holiness Mission and the Church of the Nazarene. J. B. Maclagan had gone in 1945 to be superintendent minister of the I.H.M. and pastor of the Thomas Memorial Church in London, a move that had been seriously misunderstood by some of Maclagan's former colleagues. Indeed, George Frame saw the move as a betrayal, similar to that of Robert Purvis, who had finally gone to the United Free Church of Scotland. Others felt that the I.H.M. was a sister denomination and, as Arthur Fawcett had moved from the International Holiness Mission to the Church of the Nazarene, so Maclagan was moving into the ranks of the I.H.M. Of course, Maclagan was highly regarded and his going was a serious blow to the church. He declared later that his intention had always been to establish the foundation for such a union as took place in 1952.

Union almost doubled the financial support which churches gave to the college. The International Holiness Mission had twenty-seven churches and almost 1,000 members in Britain at the time of union and another eighteen hundred members in Africa. In addition, this made the idea of union with the Calvary Holiness Church more feasible, and when by 1955 the three Holiness bodies were united under the Church of the Nazarene, the future of the college was no longer in doubt. Frame had indeed been a man of faith, and what seemed like folly in 1943 was now confirmed as far-sighted vision.

Chapter 3

THE STRUGGLE TO SURVIVE

As I reflect on these post-war years it becomes evident that the story of the survival of Hurlet Nazarene College reflects the faith and faithfulness of the people called Nazarenes. The minutes of Trustee meetings held during this time suggest the chronic need for financial assistance, a situation not fully appreciated by the members of the denomination. All were anxious to have a trained ministry but the establishing of college budgets was a slow and sometimes painful business. Of course, most of the churches were themselves small and struggling. There was constant pressure on them for increased giving to support their own local needs.

The employment of a regular paid staff was out of the question. Men like Revd David Anderson and Revd Peter Clark came to the college on minimal remuneration. The Clarks, who, after a lifetime of service in the church, gave the closing years of ministry to the college, were paid £3 per week, plus room and board. Even that was a strain on resources.

I recall that feeding students was equally difficult in those post-war years. Rationing was occasionally augmented by C.A.R.E. packages from the United States. There was a large garden in which students were expected to work each afternoon, but apart from fruit and potatoes the garden gave very little produce. When, in 1945, men began to be released from the forces, a Canadian serviceman, Howard Duckering, from Red Deer, came to Hurlet to care for the grounds. Among other things he purchased a milking cow, "Blossom," who supplied us with milk until sold by Revd Peter Clark. Prayer and fasting was a valuable practice in those days as it helped out on the budget and on meals! Of course, during the war most people were on a limited diet, so restrictions at college were seen in a different light. Indeed, as I write and recall our student years from 1946 to 1948, I do not remember ever feeling that we did not have enough to eat, although there were times when greater variety would have been appreciated!

It is with affection that I reflect on West Hurlet House and its facilities. The building had some 18 rooms of various size. A large entrance hall connected an open lounge (later to be enclosed as a lecture room and meeting room) to the former drawing room, panelled in dark oak. A corridor led to an annexe to the main building, and on the right was a small lounge used as an office. Further along the corridor were several pantries, one of which was re-designed as a student communal wash-room. Kitchen, butler's pantry and dining room were further along this corridor. A narrow stairway led up to the first floor of the annexe and here were six bedrooms, which held bunk beds for sixteen male students.

A wide stair led from the hall to the first floor; half-way up was a large conservatory. The first floor had two large south-facing rooms (the college library and the Principal's sitting room) and two north facing rooms used as family bedrooms. Apart from the library, this first floor was the private accommodation for the Principal and his family. The second floor had four bedrooms and two bathrooms for staff and for female students.

At the main Barrhead Road entrance to the grounds was a small four-roomed cottage, at first used as a manse by the Paisley church, and later used for married student housing. From the main entrance a wide avenue ran some 300 yards to the main building. Another avenue of similar length led to the rear Paisley Road entrance. Nestling at the side of the main building was a small cottage and coach house, the latter used as book-room and furnace room, and the former as a manse for the pastor of the Govan church.

Photo No 7
Cottage and Garage

All was set in ten acres of land, containing a large fruit and vegetable garden, an old disused tennis court and lawns with a large greenhouse. The previous owner had paid little attention to the grounds, one of the features of which was undoubtedly the splendid rhododendron bushes which, in spring, had a variety of blossoms, quite exceptional and breathtaking in their beauty. The grounds were surrounded on all sides by farmland and in a sense were rather isolated, the nearest neighbour being 500 yards away.

The purchase of this property was a monumental act of faith. How to furnish and maintain it was a further test of the commitment of the churches to the project. There were one or two antique pieces left, but the furnishing of the house was to be done piecemeal over some years and from a number of sources. Everything was obtained in the early years from private donors or auction rooms. A member of the Uddingston church, Miss E. S. L. Baxter, procured a large amount of carpeting which had already had twenty years of wear on the floor of a busy restaurant. The college was able to acquire this and the lounge, library, stairs and other places were carpeted with it. One large section was brought to England in 1958, when the college moved, and, thirty years later, was still in service on the floor of the attic in Manchester, worn but stubbornly surviving. Those sixty years of life speak well for Templeton carpets!

Beds were a necessity, of course, and the college purchased iron bunks and bedding from the army surplus. Some of the blankets still linger, pressed into service now as packing blankets or car-boot liners. Wardrobes were non-existent in those early years. Students used open cupboards with curtains drawn across them. The lounge was initially used as a dining room, with students sitting around a large refectory table. Desks were not purchased until the early 1950s when tables of all sorts were replaced by specially manufactured desks, each an extravagant purchase at £3!

During this time everybody with furniture to discard would send it to the college. One can guess that it was a hotch-potch, but we never seemed to care too much in those days. Of course, most of us came from working-class homes where matching furniture was more of a dream than a reality. Floor covering was scarce in some rooms but gradually floors were covered with linoleum.

To feed staff and students from one small cooker was difficult. The installation of an Esse stove (which also heated water for bathrooms) was a great step forward. The ladies who came to work as cooks certainly did not come for the money or the up-to-date facilities. For them it was, without doubt, a desire to serve God and the church. The truth of the matter is that the budget for housekeeping in those days was s-t-r-e-t-c-h-e-d far beyond what seemed possible, thus suggesting that God was helping in many ways to keep the doors of Hurlet Nazarene College open.

When the General N.Y.P.S. decided to sponsor Hurlet as their project after the 1948 General Convention in St. Louis they were not to know how critical this support would prove. The capital indebtedness was in itself a heavy burden. Private loans of one kind or another had made the purchase possible but the repayment of these was difficult. The problem was compounded by the fact that early in 1948 dry rot was discovered in the fabric of the main building, a greater problem than at first suspected. The roof to the annexe had been leaking for some time and this had aggravated the situation. The college was faced with a major repair, which was a daunting prospect, and led to some debate over retaining the property. There can be little doubt but that this development meant sleepless nights for George Frame. The cost of the work was finally to be as much as 50% of the original purchase price.

It was at this juncture that the N.Y.P.S. launched their project to raise $10,000 to clear the original indebtedness. How to take care of the cost of repairs was another matter and several schemes were devised to help in this. A minute from a meeting held on January 3rd, 1949, stated with regard to the repair:

The District Superintendent reviewed the repair work being done in the college, on the roof and the interior, the cost of which he hoped to raise by Easter, 1949, by personal solicitations[8]. It was evident that there was a great need to raise this money in order to pay the building contractor. A letter from Dr Lauriston DuBois, Executive Secretary of the Nazarene Young People's Society, suggested that the Commonwealth representative on the General N.Y.P.S. Council, T. E. Martin, should make a presentation of the money raised on the occasion of his visit to Britain. Almost $5,000 had already been paid. The Nazarene Publishing House was also raising funds to help with the establishing of a bookroom at the college. The Board of Trustees sent a request to Nazarene Headquarters in Kansas City, that in view of the devaluation of the pound, recently announced by Sir Stafford Cripps, the new exchange rate be the basis of the final payments. This was finally accepted and of course meant that the total indebtedness on the building and on the repair work was practically cleared.

Photo No 8
Dr Ted Martin presenting cheque for $10,000

This was a vital factor in the future life of the college and it seemed that the hand of God was upon the work in this matter.

The encouragement which these gifts gave was tremendous, and imparted a sense of optimism about the college to the Church of the Nazarene in Britain. In the minutes of a meeting held on 23rd September, 1949, the value of this generous gift was summed up thus:

It was estimated that owing to the liberal offering received from the General N.Y.P.S.. about $1,500 would be available to assist in the purchase of:
1. An "Esse" Stove,
2. Linoleum for Annexe Hall,
3. Wardrobes for student rooms. 9

In addition, the acceptance of the college as one of the institutions of Higher Education meant that the General Church of the Nazarene made an small annual grant to the college which was to be of great assistance over the years. Clearly a new day was dawning and the lessening pressures of capital indebtedness meant that the day-to-day running of the college would be more easily undertaken.

In view of the financial pressure on the college the fees might well have been increased. From 1945 to 1950 these had been set and maintained at £40 per three term session. This included tuition, room, and board. Of course, this amount looks ludicrous now, but in those days it was high enough to be daunting. When I entered college in April 1946, my wife and I had saved £120 over the previous five years. That was to be used to furnish our first home, but was now set aside for fees for three years in college. No educational grants were given, yet after three years in college and a further three in university, when we came back to college to teach we had exactly £120 and sixpence in our bank account, all our fees paid and a considerable amount of furniture in our home.

When the fees were raised (in March 1951) to £60 per year it was stated that every effort would be made by the Trustees to furnish scholarships for students facing hardship. It was only in the early fifties that local authorities in Scotland began to award discretionary grants to students. The fees were not increased again until 1954 when they were raised to £90 per year. The total receipts in the academic year 1952-53 were £1,500. This was to feed students, pay staff, and take care of overheads. That year we showed a balance in the current account, which we continued to do for the next fourteen years.

The fact is that it was only with the help of the Lord, wise planning and a great deal of sacrifice on the part of students and staff that we managed to survive the pressures of that first decade, 1944-54. We did not eat lamb but we always enjoyed our leg of mutton for Sunday lunch! Hurlet may not have been a so-called "Faith college" but again and again it was only by faith that the whole enterprise was maintained.

Chapter 4

MUCH ADO ABOUT NOTHING

Funding and feeding were not the only problems faced during this first decade of college life. Questions were being raised about the condition of the building and in particular the soundness of the foundations. The fact that the property was surrounded by old mine workings caused some to question the desirability of retaining the property. At a meeting of the Trustees held in Parkhead Church on 20th January, 1949, the following minute was recorded:

A meeting was held at which the District Superintendent [Dr George Frame] *read a letter from Brother Victor Edwards* [Dr Sharpe's son-in-law] *regarding the condition of the building. Brother Frame explained that the major portion of the trouble was not dry rot but dampness from the roof. He submitted a quotation of £94 for installing central heating in the annexe. It was felt that this was a reasonable offer and would be better done while the present repair work was proceeding. It was agreed to accept the quotation.*[10]

While this might have been the end of the criticism, it was in fact all that was needed to begin what came to be a running saga over several months. The matter of the suitability of the property was raised at the District Assembly and the delegates requested "that a full investigation be made by the college Trustees into allegations concerning the college property."[11]

It was then decided by the Trustees, meeting in April, 1949, that such an investigation should take place at the college on 14th May, 1949. Several building specialists were included in the investigating committee. The meeting took place on the 14th May and the Executive met on the 15th to discuss the report. The members present were Dr George Frame, Revd

Fletcher Tink and Revd Sydney Martin, and Messrs. Walter Neil and Victor Edwards. Also present were Mr Tom Pritchard, one of the consultants, and Mr Henderson, representing the building company of Messrs. Maclaren.

Mr Henderson, with the help of Brother Pritchard made an examination of the building and declared that, in his (Mr Henderson's) *estimation, the evidences of subsidence were such as might be reasonably expected having regard to the age of the building. He further stated that the effects were not the result of underground workings and that the condition of the structure was generally sound. He agreed to submit a written statement to this effect.*

Some discussion followed and arising out of this ...

Mr Frame read a report of an examination which had been held in May 1935 for the information of the owners certifying that there were no underground working beneath the college premises.[12]

Brother Edwards arrived late and being made aware of the report a second examination of the building was made. After this Brother Edwards still expressed doubts as to the condition of the building. A further consultation was proposed with the previous owner. A report was given on the matter at a meeting of Trustees (Executive) held at Hurlet Nazarene College on 27th June, 1949. The full Executive was present and the following minute recorded:

In consequence of enquiries made regarding cost and nature of major repairs upon the house executed by former owners, Brother Frame reported that he had interviewed a Mr Wilson who had been the owner and occupant of West Hurlet House from approximately 1912 to 1928. Mr Wilson, before purchasing, had called in a representative of Messrs. McReady and Stevenson of Glasgow, to conduct a thorough examination of house and grounds, and had subsequently purchased the whole of the grounds and property on the strength of the report of the inspection.

In 1918 Mr Wilson had had the floors on the ground floor renewed at an approximate cost of £400. He stated that, to his knowledge, the wall tie was in position before the year 1910.

Brother Edwards maintained that, in his opinion, it would be advisable to sell West Hurlet House now before its value on the market depreciated further. He made the suggestion that an available house be purchased at the coast which, besides being used as a college during the session, could be used as a guest house in the holiday season.

After some discussion it was suggested by Brother Frame that he and Brother Edwards make statements of their respective cases to the Board of Trustees in September. This suggestion was sustained by the Committee. [13]

Thus the story continued and one cannot but ask the question: did Mr Edwards have real grounds for his unwillingness to accept the assessment of the committee in face of the evidence? In other areas he and Frame did not see eye to eye and this may have made him more reluctant to accept the verdict. While there was no suggestion that Frame had any other interests than those of the college and the church, his method of reporting the use of funds was not always accepted by some members of the District. But Edwards, while critical of Frame in regard to the matters of finance, was himself anxious to safeguard the church from serious financial loss if there should be serious structural problems. At the meeting held on November, 1949, the following was recorded:

The meeting now proceeded to the main business and Brother Frame suggested that such business might be expedited if the following procedure was observed:
(1) The making of statements by Brother Edwards and himself.
(2) The withdrawal of Brother Edwards and himself subject to further information being required by the remaining trustees.
(3) Discussion and presenting of recommendation by remaining trustees...
The report from the investigative committee was requested and read from the minutes.

Statement by Brother Edwards:
Brother Edwards denied that he had stated that the foundation of the college was undermined, but he insisted that the fabric of the building was unsound due to the presence of nearby workings and dry rot. In view of this fact, and especially bearing in mind that owing to the liberality of the General N.Y.P.S., the necessity for wise stewardship on the part of the trustees had been increased, he considered that the college premises should be sold at once. Such a sale would certainly result in a heavy financial loss but even this was to be preferred to the possibility of being faced with the burdens of heavy and recurring major repairs.

In addition to this, and having in mind the need for operating a long term policy, it would be wise to purchase suitable property at the coast which could be used in the nature of a Christian guest house during the summer months. Referring to the civil engineer's report as to the soundness of the building Brother Edwards stated that, in his opinion, their present worth was doubtful because mining records were not accurately kept until comparatively recent times. To retain the present premises was like pouring money into a sieve.

Statement by Brother Frame:
Brother Frame read a letter which he had received from Brother Edwards in January and relating to the advisability of disposing of the present college building.

A letter from Mrs Pirie, the last owner of the house, was read together with an enclosed report from the civil engineer which testified to the general soundness of West Hurlet at the time when Mrs Pirie was contemplating purchasing. Reference was made by Brother Frame to a verbal report received by him from Mr Wilson, an earlier owner of the house, which also declared that the house was in sound condition. Mr Wilson had mentioned that he had renewed the floors on the ground level.

Brother Frame went on to sum up his case as follows:

The condition of the house itself. He considered that on the strength of the reports available from experts there was every reason for believing that the house was in reasonably sound condition. The preliminary examinations of the house, prior to purchase by the District, had not revealed the presence of dry rot. Had there been the slightest grounds for suspecting this condition, which unfortunately had revealed itself subsequently, the property would certainly not have been purchased. As it was, every precaution had been taken to deal with the dry rot, though of course, no guarantee could be given that the trouble had been permanently cured.

Suspected subsidence. There had undoubtedly been movement at some time but investigation had resulted in the conclusion that having reference to the age of the building, such movement was due to normal settlement.

Alleged unsuitability of present site. The decision to purchase Hurlet had not been hastily arrived at. One factor which had been taken into account at the time was its central location in relation to the bulk of the churches. Had a house at the coast been available at the time it would have been considered. The idea of using college premises as a boarding house in the summer months was not necessarily practicable, in view of staff problems and other factors. The use of Hurlet as a guest house, in a somewhat modified form, was being, and had always been, kept in mind[14].

This discussion between Edwards and Frame had taken up considerable time and effort. The matter appears, in retrospect, and in light of the above minutes to have had more to do with leadership and policy than with the actual problem raised. One cannot help but reflect that in other areas the relations between these two men were at best uneasy. This inevitably influenced the whole discussion and the feeling is not easily dismissed that the question of the suitability of the college building, while it had some part to play in the discussion, was rather being used to make life more difficult for Frame and his supporters. Indeed, Edwards went on to say at this same meeting, "that brother Frame's statement had contained no declaration of policy for the college." Edwards concluded by declaring emphatically that the college, at present, was a white elephant.

The remainder of the Board discussed the whole matter. The result was that they unanimously supported Frame in terms of the soundness of the building and in its location. They made a gesture to Edwards by suggesting that, "... in view of the seriousness of the allegations made, the up-to-date testimony of an expert be procured."[15] A statement was to be prepared for presentation to the next District Assembly.

Whatever the reason for Edwards' opposition, he had succeeded in creating a measure of uncertainty in the minds of many church members. It is true that subsidence in certain parts of the grounds was in evidence. Indeed for several years prior to leaving Hurlet we dumped our refuse, which was not collected by the authorities, into a large hole which had appeared in a part of the grounds, and was referred to as "the bottomless pit." This would suggest that Edwards had some evidence of the movement caused by the workings underground, but this was fifty yards or more from the building. In 1958 Hurlet was sold and still stands occupied and further developed.

By 1950 the college was on the way to becoming an integral part in the life of the church. If the discussions about the property achieved anything of value it was to give the people called Nazarenes a readiness to assume more responsibility for the upkeep of the property. As is so often the case, this *cause célèbre* created a great interest and in consequence the support which had been slow in coming was hastened by the controversy. Frame's case was further strengthened by the fact that in 1952 conversations being held between the leaders of the International Holiness Mission and those of the Church of the Nazarene were about to be concluded in the union of both groups under the banner of the international Church of the Nazarene. This meant a greater need for trained ministry and a broader base for support. Within eight years of the first unimpressive beginnings the college administration had weathered the storm of a major repair and major dispute as to college viability, and the course seemed set fair for the future role of the college in the life of the church.

Photo No 9
Students and Staff 1951

*Photo No 10
Professor Kenneth Grider and students
in the lecture room at Hurlet.*

*Photo No 11
Manual Work at Hurlet on a foggy afternoon,
Revd Peter Clark Supervising.*

48 *Scholarship on fire*

Photo No 12
Union with I.H.M. Leeds, 1952

Photo No 13
Staff and Students, Hurlet, 1957

Much ado about nothing 49

Photo No 14
*1957 Graduation in Paisley. Speaker: Revd D. W. Lambert
Principal of Lebanon Bible College*

Photo No 15
*Summer Evangelistic team
L-R Alex Jones, John Crouch, Hugh Rae, Cyril Frame*

50   Scholarship on fire

Photo No 16
Farewell Gathering with Paisley Church of the Nazarene Board, April, 1958.

Chapter 5

CHANGE IN LEADERSHIP

Though George Frame served as Principal until 1954, it was inevitably a part-time responsibility, since his duties as District Superintendent often called him away from the college. This meant that it was essential for others to assume oversight in his absence. At first men like John Walker and John Mitchell were employed to carry out the every day running of the college. Neither man was an academic and therefore matters which affected academic development were not always given the attention and the priority they required. In addition, the authority carried by these men was not clearly spelt out, resulting in conflict between staff and students.

The fact that both these men left the college after such brief tenures serves to underscore the difficulties and frustrations of this kind of arrangement. In the long term this situation would have undermined the disciplines of college life. The pressure was also felt by students, particularly those older students who wanted to make the most of these years. This meant that the attrition rate was greater than need have been, especially among serious-minded students.

Subsequent assistants were Revd David Anderson and Revd Peter Clark, men of mature years. However, although Clark had been a student in George Sharpe's first college and Anderson a student in the college at Motherwell in 1926, both were unfamiliar with educational needs and practices of the late 1940s. Though Clark functioned as both Dean and Business Manager, decision-making was always subject to the approval of the Principal, who was often absent. The results of this dual leadership were not very satisfactory. Class work was not always as systematic as it should have been, and discipline was somewhat haphazard, since these older men were at times unaware of developing problems.

In the seven years since the first classes had met, the Board of Trustees had always kept before them the need for a full-time Principal. It had been hoped that the Department of Education at the international offices of the Church of the Nazarene in Kansas City might have been able to suggest someone, but that had not come about. The practical issues of salary and housing were no doubt something of a deterrent. The name of Dr A. E. Collins was given consideration. He had served briefly as President of Canadian Nazarene College and had planned a visit to Britain. That visit never materialised and that matter was taken no further. With the departure of Kenneth Grider and the retirement of Peter Clark, it was evident that new and more permanent staff were required. The development of the curriculum now required lecturers with academic preparation. But where was one to look for such people?

1952 was the year of the General Assembly of the Church of the Nazarene (held every four years) and George Frame was in Kansas City for that event. It was reasonable that since Kenneth Grider had made such a fine contribution to the college, Frame would invite someone with similar plans to come to Britain and, while studying, give time to teaching and supervision. Several couples were interviewed by Frame at this time but there seemed to be no one available to come under this kind of arrangement.

I was at that time the District Nazarene Young People's President. I had graduated from Hurlet Nazarene College at Christmas 1948, pastored for several months in Dundee and in October, 1949, had enrolled at the University of Glasgow in a programme leading to the Master of Arts degree. Already ordained by the British Isles District in 1949, I was now beginning to make plans for the future. I had been approached by another Nazarene college to consider joining the staff but declined to do that on the basis that I wanted to work in Britain if possible, and hoped to combine pastoring with teaching at Hurlet College. As District N.Y.P.S. President I had been elected as a delegate to the 1952 General Convention of the N.Y.P.S. in Kansas City. We were all aware of the fact that Dr Frame was interviewing couples who might be interested in Britain. I was not in the least surprised at this.

During the General Assembly delegates and visitors from the British Isles would often get together for an evening snack, usually at the Katz Drug Store. On one of these occasions, Dr Frame, Revd J. S. Logan and I were talking about the day's events at the Assembly. Suddenly, out of the blue, Dr Frame looked across the table and said, "Hugh, how old are you?" I answered that I was 31. That was the end of that part of the conversation. We continued with the meal and then went to our respective hotel rooms. I was sharing a room with J. S., who later in the evening asked me what George Frame's question was about. I put him off with some answer, but in my mind I had already figured out the import of the question. It seemed to me that George Frame, who had known me since my boyhood (and still saw me as one of his students) had suddenly seen me in a different light. I was in the USA for a further two months preaching, and returned home at the end of August.

The minutes of the Board of Trustees of 19th August, 1952, at a special meeting of the Executive which included Dr Frame, Revd J. Macleod and Revd S. Martin, brothers W. Neil and W. A. Noble, show the following :

In view of Revd Peter Clark's retirement from the post of Business Manager the Executive discussed the appointment of a Dean.

Discussion led to the following motion, made by Brother Neil, seconded by Revd S. Martin and carried unanimously: *That, Revd Hugh Rae be invited to take over the position of Dean for one year with the definite thought that should this appointment be mutually satisfactory, Brother Rae be recommended to the Board of Trustees for appointment as Principal to take complete charge from the opening of the 1953 session.* [16]

The brief question in Kansas City on that June evening, had led to this invitation to become Dean. My wife Nan and I were not immediately sure that this was what we ought to do. Not that I disliked the idea, but I had seen others come to the task and quickly grow discouraged and disillusioned. My fear was that I would not be allowed to implement the changes which I sensed (as a former student) needed to be made. In the end we decided to give ourselves a year in which to find out if it could work. The prospect of being Principal was a frightening one and I was not certain that I could fill the role. I had a feeling that I was being invited because there was no one else. I was to learn many years later that that had never been the case.

We moved to Hurlet in September, 1952, only two weeks before the new college year began. I was to assume responsibility for the teaching of Systematic Theology and care for the general day-to-day running of the college.

I am sure that the students of that first year - amongst whom were Leslie Evans and Brian Farmer, who were to become leading pastors in the church - had more Moral Philosophy than Theology! A number of the students were older than I and many of them knew me on a personal basis as the N.Y.P.S. President. We had been on a first name footing but I do not recall any problems in that area. The respect I was given during those first years when I was the "new boy on the block" is one of the memories which has remained precious to me over the years. These students have been very special friends and colleagues for forty years now and to them I owe a debt of gratitude because they helped me find fulfilment through their patience and understanding.

As everybody knows, a new broom sweeps clean. I was no exception and immediately on assuming responsibility for the general running of the college, I set about planning the life of the college in a manner which would mean sharing in the responsibility for the wellbeing of the school. Discipline had formed a very important part in bringing me to this point. Leaving school at fifteen with no certificates was one of the foolish decisions my parents allowed me to make. Thus, when God finally impressed on me that I should prepare for service, there was a great amount of ground to reclaim. During the Second World War, I became increasingly aware of the need to set things in motion. I began work on the Home Study course in 1940 and, after passing a few examinations in this way, I was encouraged to think about preparing for matriculation with the University of London. That began several years of study with Wolsey Hall Correspondence College, Oxford, a course which required dedication and discipline. Rising each morning at 3 a.m. and studying until 7 a.m. before going off to work is a way of life which does not commend itself to everyone, but it allowed me to gain my matriculation and finally, encouraged by Arthur Fawcett, I entered the University of Glasgow in 1949.

When, therefore, I came to the college, I was conscious of the fact that the discipline of time and mind had been important elements in preparing me to do God's will. Forty years have not changed my mind on that; rather they have served to convince me further of the truth of this idea. But in those first months, I was impatient of any who would not discipline themselves to the needs of the task to which they had been called.

In consequence, my first year as Dean was one in which I had to learn that whatever the value of discipline, it needed to be tempered with mercy: a hard lesson to learn, but essential. The fact that the entire student body did not rise up in revolt was due, I think, to two facts. One was that most were serious students and the discipline was therefore not necessarily so irksome. The second was that most of them knew that we did care about them and that we would surely learn, as I think we did.

What about our fears that we might not have freedom to initiate change? The truth is that I was soon aware of the fact that the Principal, Dr Frame, was not only willing, but eager for me to introduce change in many areas of college life.

We came to the college in mid-September of 1952, and at the end of October the union between the International Holiness Mission and the Church of the Nazarene was completed in Leeds. During that time George Frame and Dr Mary Tanner were united in marriage. (Emily Frame had died in 1950 after a protracted fight with cancer). The plan was that Dr Tanner would sell her house and that the newly married couple would move into the college. Windows were measured for curtains. Suddenly Mrs Frame announced that they did not plan to move. That decision was probably prompted by a number of factors. The wisdom of this was evident when in April, 1954, I was elected Principal. I personally think that Dr Mary Frame saw this coming and sensed that it would be wiser to remain where they were. In all the years that I was associated with the college, George Frame gave me every support. I know that I made some decisions with which he would not have been in complete agreement, but never once in all the years did I get any sense of criticism from him. The result was that both Nan and I felt a sense of security in our work which was important to us.

As the first decade saw the establishment of the college, the second saw upheaval and change. Union with the International Holiness Mission brought into the Church of the Nazarene some 28 congregations. This meant that support for the college was increased and the potential for the student body to grow was heightened. Following the union the British Isles District was divided into "British Isles North" and "British Isles South".

In 1955 the Calvary Holiness Church united with the Church of the Nazarene, finalising the union of the three main Holiness bodies in Britain. The Calvary Holiness Church College, Beech Lawn, which had struggled over the eight years of its existence, had four students at the time of union. Two graduated prior to union and the other two, Ronald Betts and Charles Clarke, came to Hurlet to continue their studies.

The new problem confronting us concerned the location of a college for the united Holiness church. Inevitably there was indecision and discussion. The merits of Hurlet and Beech Lawn were discussed from every angle. Former Calvary Holiness Church members on the Board saw Beech Lawn as much more central to the work of the church in Britain and therefore viewed their campus with greater favour. Those previously in the Church of the Nazarene felt that the Hurlet campus, which was much larger than Beech Lawn, would be better. The Board of General Superintendents was asked for guidance and they suggested that both campuses should be sold and a new location sought.

In spite of the uncertainty of the years between 1955 and 1958 the development of the college curriculum was a pressing matter. With little financial resource, getting teachers was always something of a problem. Up to this point most of the teaching had been carried out by local pastors living within travelling distance of the college. All of these were busy pastors with the ability, but mostly without the time to develop a strong academic programme.

In 1952 an American, Mary Mellinger, came to live at the college and taught English. When she finally returned to the United States another teacher came to us - Miss Olive Bangs, sister to two other church theologians, Dr Mildred Wynkoop and Dr Carl Bangs. Olive came with excellent credentials and while she was with us taught N.T. Greek and Biblical Studies. She moved with us to Beech Lawn in April, 1958, but was suddenly called back to the USA on account of her mother's illness. While the college was still at Hurlet, Revd Sydney Martin, Revd David J. Tarrant, Revd Jock T. Henson, Revd William Henson, Revd Stanley Tranter, Revd T. Crichton Mitchell, Miss Margaret K. Latta (retired missionary), and Mrs Jean Pollock were amongst those who taught. They were a committed group of people who, while carrying other responsibilities in the church, gave ungrudgingly of their time and talent.

My preparation for this leadership role into which I had been called was in some ways ample but in others meagre. At seventeen I had been involved in church leadership, first at the local level and then on the District. These responsibilities had developed some skills of leadership, although at every level I was to suffer personally for many years from a feeling of inadequacy in that capacity. In fact this led in 1956 to my suggesting that at the end of a two year contract the Board of Trustees should feel free to appoint as Principal Revd Jack Ford, formerly Principal of Beech Lawn, under whom I would serve (if he so wished). Events were to follow a course which kept me in the Principal's chair until I resigned from the college in June, 1966.

In other ways my preparation for this kind of leadership of an educational institution was basically nil. I had no formal training in administration, none in accountancy and had not been exposed to the influence of similar colleges either within or outwith the denomination. I could have done with a ready-made pack of instructions. In addition to these difficulties was the fact that there was no clear philosophy of education worked out for the college.

We had pastors whose training had been in Emmanuel Missionary Training College, and some who were products of the Faith Mission College, both being institutions which tried to follow a very strict code of conduct. On the other hand the experience we had of graduates from our North American colleges suggested a more liberal approach. All kinds of strange expectations were afloat. Conflicting advice as to how the college should be run was always available. The truth is that in these years of transition it became increasingly evident that we must work our way through to a philosophy which would help us to produce not spoon-fed graduates, but rather men and women who would develop their minds in such a way that they would gain confidence in the handling of the Word of God on a sound exegetical basis and also develop leadership techniques which would make them leaders of others.

We still, however, faced serious needs in terms of the development of the college. Only by finding a more sound financial base would we be able to begin the long haul towards the goal of acceptable scholarship. This goal was to be kept in mind over the coming three decades. It was a goal which was to demand a total rebuilding of the philosophy of ministry which we would need to embrace if we would fulfil our obligations both to the young people who would come to the college, and to the church which looked to us for a supply of pastors.

George Frame had certainly envisaged a college which would offer the best in scholarship. The vision was there, but how was it to be realised unless major steps were taken with regard to full-time teaching staff? It was one thing to develop a philosophy of education for the college; quite another matter to bring about the necessary changes. My vision on taking office in 1954 was to have at least three full-time lecturers; it was my conviction that the future of theological education (and ministerial preparation) would be secured only when scholars could be found who would be willing to invest in the college despite its paucity of financial resources.

In 1958, Alex Deasley, son of a Nazarene minister, graduated with his BA in New Testament from the University of Cambridge. In 1957 the Board of Trustees unanimously agreed to write to Mr Deasley inviting him to join the college staff on completion of his degree. In the September meeting of 1958 the formal decision was taken to employ Mr Deasley, who would begin a three year contract as of October 1959. This was, of course, a major step forward for the college and was the beginning of the growth and development of staff so essential to the future.

Alex Deasley could have gone to other colleges within the church and found greater financial returns for himself and his family. Instead he continued an association with the college which had begun in 1953, when he had enrolled as a student at Hurlet, prior to his proceeding to Cambridge. This meant that Biblical Studies, so essential to ministry, was being taught by one who was already manifesting the scholarship which was to take him finally to the highest teaching institution in the Church of the Nazarene, Nazarene Theological Seminary. So began an association with the college which was to have a profound effect on the programme of the college and a tremendous influence on the church in Britain.

Photo No 17
Revd Maynard G. James, first Principal, Beech Lawn Bible College.

Chapter 6

BEECH LAWN BIBLE COLLEGE

The growth patterns of the Calvary Holiness Church, so remarkable in the early years of the denomination from 1934 to 1940, had changed quite dramatically during the Second World War. The method of evangelism seemed to remain the same, namely, outreach tent campaigns which led to the establishing of churches, but in fact those years saw the church begin to consolidate its programme. With the end of the war in 1945 many hoped that there would be a considerable extension of the work but, as Ford notes, "These hopes were only partially realised."[17]

In 1947, discussions with the Church of the Nazarene about joint responsibility for a theological college had been taking place. Then Hurlet was recognised as a Nazarene College of Higher Education. The resulting discussions led to the founding of Beech Lawn Bible College, at Uppermill, Cheshire, to train ministerial students for the Calvary Holiness Church.

In the November-December, 1946 issue of *The Flame*, the C.H.C. magazine, an article by Maynard G. James entitled "Moving Forward! The C.H.C. Bible School," contained the following statement:

After years of prayer and preparation the Calvary Holiness Church Bible School has become a reality. Through the vision and generosity of two of God's saints premises have been purchased in Uppermill, near Oldham, for the purpose of training young men for whole-time full salvation ministry. The first term will commence in January, 1947 (D.V.); and it is expected that a training course of at least two years will be drawn up for the students. The Curriculum will include such subjects as :-

The Bible - Book by Book
Theology
Church History
Evangelism
Homiletics
English Grammar and New Testament Greek

Along with these studies will be a course of "applied Christianity," such as, open-air meetings, house-to-house visitation, manual work, weekend preaching appointments, trekking and team evangelism, etc.

Already a number of young men have applied to enter the C.H.C. Bible College. There are a limited number of vacancies left. The Bible School is not confined to C.H.C. members, but as far as possible, the door is open to suitable applicants from all denominations. It must be clearly understood, however, that all students must be prepared to live a life of strict discipline in prayer, study and team work.[18]

The Flame for March/April, 1947 reported the official opening of the college on Wednesday, February 11th, 1947. It was an exciting occasion. The term had commenced with seven students and the lecturers included Revd Cyril Pass, Revd Maurice Winterburn, Revd Leonard Ravenhill, and Pastors Morell, Sabine and Gutteridge.

Uppermill was a small village situated in a beautiful part of the Pennines. It was within easy reach by bus, train or road of Manchester (15 miles) and Leeds (36 Miles). It was felt that this gave it a unique position as a base for gaining practical experience in preaching and evangelistic work.

The curriculum was much more practical than academic and in consequence leaned more heavily on the experience of the lecturers than on their academic qualifications. In many respects it was not unlike the situation which would be found in other colleges, and, like Hurlet, it depended heavily on the input of nearby ministers, in this case from the International Holiness Mission and the Calvary Holiness Church. Others also helped, such as Revd S. May, Vicar of Godley, who came to teach New Testament Greek.

It was a small beginning, but it was a recognition of the fact that training was essential for ministry. Training was the emphasis and whatever developments might be anticipated at the point of founding, the practical development of the student for ministry was seen as important. The devotional life was given a large place in the programme of the college and the students, like those at Hurlet, had little time for in-depth study. A further factor of note was that while Hurlet began with a three year course, Beech Lawn planned only two years of study.

The financial basis of the college was dependent upon the good-will of people. In the article, "Moving Forward", Maynard James says,

We are not prepared to beg for money for the necessary equipment of the Bible School. We are convinced that if God's people will pray for us, then the Holy Spirit will tell them what to do about financial support. [19]

In addition to this faith basis, students were expected to "pray in £16 per term towards their support." Tuition was deemed to be free, and whilst the amount did not cover the total costs, they relied on God to meet the needs. As with Hurlet, so Beech Lawn was launched on something of a shoe string. There were at least two substantial gifts but, unlike Hurlet, there was no larger denomination upon which to call in times of crisis.

There were early discouragements for the leaders of the college and it seemed as though the forces of the enemy would destroy this fledgling institution. Writing about these discouragements in *The Flame,* the Principal, Revd Maynard James, noted:

It sounds fine in theory to regard certain Satanic onslaughts as compliments; but in practice they reduce the saints to heart-searching and tearful supplications before the Throne of Grace. Such was the case at Beech Lawn College. But the memory of that grand opening night last year - when the glory of God descended and we burst into the joyful singing of the chorus, "A mighty revival is coming this way" - never left us. It encouraged us to hold on in prayer for deliverance from the skies. And, of course, the God who had commenced the college work answered in His own marvellous way.

The past three months have witnessed a marked advance. The increasing number of students compelled us to seek for much larger accommodation. Right on time, ideal premises in a splendid location were secured and the former building was disposed of satisfactorily.[20]

This larger property on Mottram Road, Stalybridge, Cheshire was bought. It consisted of a main red brick building and one other separate building standing in a two acre site. Maynard James writes,

The first term in the new college begins in a few days from the writing of this article. About 15 men students are expected in residence this term. They come to us from various Christian groups - Baptist, Methodist, Church of England, and Holiness denominations included. The Bible College Committee have asked Brother James to continue as Principal. Two new tutors are joining the staff [these were not full-time staff]. *They are Revd Jack Ford, BD, who is taking Hebrew and Church History; and Revd Clifford Filer, who will teach Theology. The Revs. Percy Hassam, C. J. Pass, and C.D. Warren will continue to give their valuable services.*[21]

By Easter, 1950, James reported an enrolment of 16 students. Of these only four belonged to the Calvary Holiness Church. Three belonged to the International Holiness Mission and the other nine were from a variety of missions and churches. The fact that there were only four students from the movement itself indicates that the expected growth was not taking place within the Calvary Holiness Church. This fact was to have a serious impact on the ultimate growth of the college. Ford says, "Ironically, the provision of a source of supply for new churches was accompanied by a decline in the effectiveness of Forward Movement evangelism." [22]

In September, 1950, Revd Jack Ford became Principal. Some eight students had graduated and there was only one new applicant enrolled. Ford introduced tuition for the London Certificate of Proficiency in Religious Knowledge and this encouraged two former students to return and seven new students to enrol in September, 1951, making an enrolment of eleven. It seemed that the future for the college was a little more hopeful, but surprisingly, Jack Ford's term as Principal saw a decline in the student intake and when, after four years, he resigned, Maynard James stepped into the breach.

It would have seemed that the one man in the denomination with academic qualifications (Ford had graduated with the Bachelor of Divinity degree from London University in 1948) would be the one who could inspire growth in the college, yet the fact is that under his leadership it did not grow as expected. This stemmed from the fact the church itself was in a changing state: the college needed a strong, growing, supportive group and the Calvary Holiness Church was not showing those signs in the early 1950s prior to union with the Church of the Nazarene. It would be unfair to judge the success of the college on the basis of leadership style; it could not to be expected that a church in some decline could expect a college to turn it around.

Had there been new growth and outreach the college would have benefited and, in turn, would have been able to produce candidates for the ministry. Here is evidence, if evidence we need, that a theological college depends for its supply of students on the growth patterns of the denomination it serves. If the excitement generated in the 1930s by the young men like James, Ford, Filer and Ravenhill, who founded the Calvary Holiness Church, could have been generated in the churches of the late 1940s and early 1950s, then the history of Beech Lawn and indeed of the Holiness Movement might well have been different.

The records of students who attended are not readily available and thus the full history of the college is not easily analysed. In correspondence with some former students it would seem likely that about forty students attended Beech Lawn Bible College during its eight year history. Most of these went back to the groups from which they had come while a number of the graduates were to serve the church in other lands. The college produced some graduates who have given faithful service to the Church of the Nazarene, including Revd Ron Thomas, Revd John Weatherill, and Revd Raymond Spence, while Revd Edward and Margaret Cairns were outstanding missionaries. The life of Beech Lawn as a separate college was brief but influential, and Jack Ford was to play a further important role in the life of the combined colleges.

Photo No 18
Beech Lawn Bible College, Uppermill, 1947-49

Photo No 19
Beech Lawn Bible College and Flat, Stalybridge

Photo No 20
Students and Staff of Beech Lawn Bible College,
Mottram Road, Stalybridge.

Photo 21
C.H.C. Ministers and families,
Beech Lawn Bible College

Chapter 7

THE DILEMMA OF LOCATION
(Uniting Two Colleges)

When union between the Calvary Holiness Church and the Church of the Nazarene took place on June 11th, 1955, the question of the future location of the college had not yet been resolved. Those who had been part of the founding of Beech Lawn Bible College and who had supported it were naturally anxious that, if possible, it be retained. On the other hand those who had been in at the beginning of Hurlet, and who had watched its development over the previous decade were equally certain that this college should continue to function in Scotland.

Those of us immediately involved in the running of the colleges were caught between the two and it was difficult, if not impossible, to be objective in assessing the situation as it really was rather than as we would have liked it to be. The campus at Hurlet was certainly larger both in terms of the physical building and in the acreage involved. There were ten acres at Hurlet as against two and a half acres at Beech Lawn, and the Beech Lawn building always seemed to be more of a private dwelling in its architectural design and size than Hurlet.

Beech Lawn's greatest asset was that it was more centrally located with respect to the new boundaries of the British Isles Church of the Nazarene than was Hurlet. Its greatest liability was the fact that internal changes would be necessary for a growing college and the amount of land was too small for long term growth.

Hurlet on the other hand was spacious and had much more ground, although it was not certain if it could be built upon. It was already successfully operating and this could not be said, at the time of union, of Beech Lawn, when there were only four students. By contrast there were twenty students in Hurlet at the time, many of whom were from England and Ireland, indicating that distance was not a serious problem.

A further factor of importance (largely overlooked by the Board of Governors) was the role that Hurlet played amongst the young people in the West of Scotland. Few students of that period can ever forget the gatherings on Friday evenings of young people from the local churches. The large lounge, which was used as a classroom, was filled each week with enthusiastic, involved young people. These gatherings at Hurlet were exciting and brought a sense of vibrancy to the work of the college so important in the lives of students and young people alike. In recalling his years spent as a student in Hurlet, Revd Hugh Gorman, now pastoring with his wife, Joan, in Red Deer, Alberta, Canada, writes, "I shall always remember the Friday night fellowship meetings..." [23]

Beech Lawn had hosted a drawing room meeting, supported by an older age group, serving a different purpose, yet greatly appreciated by those who attended. Revd John Weatherill, writing in *The Flame* about the influences of Beech Lawn on him as a student wrote: "Unforgettable impressions have been made upon me...for instance, the spiritual tone and fellowship of the Friday night drawing room meetings." [24]

A further element in the life of Hurlet was its strategic location, in the very heartland of the British Church of the Nazarene (as it was before the unions). The whole tradition of the church was centred in this area, with churches such as Parkhead, Paisley, Govan, Port Glasgow and Uddingston close enough to the college to mean that their ministry was felt by all the students. To move would mean that students as well as the young people of the larger group of churches in the West of Scotland would lose this source of fellowship.

Thus the question of location would not be easily answered and whatever the result there would be those who would feel a sense of loss - even betrayal. When the Board of Trustees met in September, 1955, the matter was very high on the agenda. The discussion which followed was one in which all participated with freedom. Many assets and liabilities were discussed. The architecture of each of the buildings was so different. One former trustee of Beech Lawn saw Hurlet as a dull, oppressive grey-stone building while those of us who had come to love that Georgian building saw Beech Lawn as plain red brick, not to be compared with the dignity of grey sandstone!

The discussion went on for hours, even days, and an impasse was reached. As Principal of Hurlet, I suggested that we place both properties on the market. One would obviously be sold first, and we would simply keep the other. It was a mischievous suggestion, since I wanted to remain in Hurlet, but I recall with some amusement the look and tone of amazement in the eyes and voice of dear Brother James, for whom this was a particularly sensitive issue. He said with no small amount of Welsh fervour, "Is that a serious suggestion, my dear brother? Everybody knows which building will sell first." He, of course, meant that it would be an unfair contest, since Beech Lawn would sell immediately, while no one would want to purchase West Hurlet. The matter was finally referred to the Board of General Superintendents for their combined judgment. When this came, it was that we should sell both properties and move to a neutral location, probably further south. Both Beech Lawn and Hurlet were placed on the market in the same month, and, ironically, Hurlet was sold eighteen months before Beech Lawn.

Nan and I paid a visit to Beech Lawn, which was still unsold, to measure the rooms and try to decide what we should bring in the event of our moving on a temporary basis to Stalybridge, where Beech Lawn was located. I made some floor plans and began to assess what should come and what should be left. On our return to Glasgow we began the task of packing and preparing to move. We had arranged for a removal company to bring three of their largest removal vans.

Prior to the move we had our final graduation service in the Paisley Church of the Nazarene. Amongst those graduating in that last class were Revd Dr Bill Stewart (now District Superintendent of Canada Atlantic District), Revd Ian Robertson (now serving the church in California), and Charles Clarke (now an Anglican minister in Cardiff). That was the last class to graduate from what had been called Hurlet Nazarene College. By the next graduation the name would have changed. It was at a meeting held in Beech Lawn in the autumn of 1958, a few months after we left Hurlet that the question of the name of the college was raised. Some, like Dr Ford, felt that we should continue to call the college Hurlet since that was the name by which it was known internationally. After some discussion it was decided to change the name to British Nazarene College. Then it was felt that we ought to call it British Isles Nazarene College and so when we moved to Didsbury that was the name adopted. Soon it was simply BINC by which it was most commonly referred to.

While we had been looking over Beech Lawn I had given each room a number on the sketch floor plans which I had made. Prior to the removal men coming I had marked on the back of each piece of furniture the room number and position of each piece after delivery. The removal firm spent most of two days getting the contents of West Hurlet House packed. It was a mammoth task. Disassembling the large oak bookcase which had housed the library was particularly difficult. This beautiful piece of Edwardian furniture from a large estate had been purchased by the District Council of the Nazarene Young People's Society, and the expert craftsmen of our Port Glasgow church had used their skills to make the furniture suit its new location. Finally all was packed and the fleet of vans moved off. As a family we followed in our car, arriving at Beech Lawn the following day. On arrival we were delighted to discover that all the furniture and furnishings had been delivered and placed in the rooms marked for them, and no major change was needed. The students, or at least some of them, had helped us in the packing and in the unpacking process, as Hugh Gorman recalls:

"...I think I should also have received a diploma in furniture moving after all our moves from Hurlet - Ashton - Beech Lawn - And then with another big Fermanagh Irishman, who thought Manual Labour was a Spanish bullfighter, moving all that furniture into The White House." [25]

What a host of memories were left behind on that April day in 1958 when the removal men started down the long avenue from Hurlet. In some ways it was to us like a burial, but then, memories such as we had could not ever be buried. I had been a student in Hurlet for almost three years. In those years I had not only been brought closer to God, I had also made friendships with lecturers and students which were to be important to me for the rest of life.

I remembered the day Dr Frame decided to learn to drive a car, with David Anderson beside him as the experienced driver. A long skid mark at the end of the Paisley drive and a stone pillar, once five foot high and two foot square, now horizontal, was the evidence of a failure to keep control. It was also a reminder of the tenacity of George Frame who, despite several failures and poor eyesight, went on to pass his driving test.

I remembered amusing student pranks common in college life. In one, some rapscallions, anticipating the late arrival of other students via the back door, had prepared a watery welcome. It was, however, the Principal who received the ablution of cold water on that occasion!

One of the very precious personal memories we had was the day a few weeks after moving into the college when Nan in her morning devotions had been given a special word from the Lord which at the time did not seem to be relevant. That Friday evening, I was called out of the gathering to the telephone to learn that Nan's mother had suddenly died. The word of the Lord then became clear and had been for her a preparation for this event.

We had been so busy that we had not seen "Ma" for several weeks. On the previous Monday evening, however, Nan had been speaking at a ladies meeting in Kilsyth, just north of Glasgow, and decided, as she travelled through the city, somewhat later than usual, to spend the night with her mother. After a chat and visit she rose in the morning, and slipping out, came home. Four days later the Lord took her mother to be with Himself; she had been a valiant servant. Then exactly one year later to within a half hour of the time of Ma's death our daughter, Marjory, was born.

As we walked for the last time around the grounds and through the house, now empty, we suddenly felt as if we were abandoning our safe haven. We were indeed going out, not knowing whither we went. Hurlet was - and in many ways remains - our first love. We have always felt that Hurlet men and women were somehow special and they have over the years formed a very intimate circle. We soon realised, however, that there could be no looking back with longing. We had to look forward to the unknown future with the certain knowledge that God would guide aright.

The future was very uncertain; we were strangers in a strange land and for a little time we were overwhelmed with homesickness. This soon passed and on our first Sunday we worshipped with our Ashton-under-Lyne friends. Their warm welcome and that of Revd and Mrs Jack Ford made us feel very much at home. As we began to unpack boxes it suddenly dawned that this was, for the moment, home, and that whatever the future held we could trust God. For one of the staff, May Kneebone, who had come from Beech Lawn as Matron, this was a homecoming. She helped us greatly to settle into our new home. That was a busy summer and we needed all the grace that God could give us. We were expecting our second child, and Peter was born in Lake Hospital, Ashton-under-Lyne on 1st December, 1958. One month later we moved, and life became nomadic.

Chapter 8

NEW DIRECTION - NEW CHALLENGE

From April until December of 1958 the home of the college was Beech Lawn. While we carried on the usual activities we were also looking for a suitable campus and trying to find a buyer for Beech Lawn.

The move itself had been complicated by the question of what to do with the books which made up the library. The library had approximately 12,000 volumes, since prior to our move from Hurlet, Dr Frame had purchased 10,000 volumes from the former Northern Congregational College for the sum of £500. Housing these volumes was something of a problem. They were delivered to Beech Lawn in the summer of 1958 and placed in the dining room, but the weight was such that we had to arrange for their removal to prevent structural damage to the building! No one, however, was around at the time to help in the housing of the books, and the dining room where the books were placed was directly above the garage thus keeping the doors from closing because of the weight.

Faced with the problem of this large consignment of books, I began to design some shelving. At the local sawmill I purchased lengths of white pine and several lengths of two by two timber and started to build shelving to house these volumes. When this shelving was in place I then spent the rest of the summer transferring the 10,000 volumes to these new shelves. Some of the volumes weighed over 10lbs, and were at least eighteen inches long by fourteen inches and six inches deep. Every day I would push more books over in a wheelbarrow and carry them up the flight of stairs, finally shelving them, not in any order but in such a way that they would not deteriorate since they were old and some of them extremely valuable.

When the students arrived in September for the beginning of the new term all was in order and college began as smoothly as if there had been no traumatic upheaval. We had a full enrolment and had a little trouble finding a place for all the returning and new students. While there was an air of uncertainty about there was also a sense of anticipation, expressed in a number of ways. That was the term when one new student was so excited that he threw his jar of Brylcream into the air, misjudging the light fixture so that the jar fell through the bowl!

At the opening service in Ashton the student involved in the Brylcream incident was testifying and recalling the event of that afternoon and suddenly said, "I was scared of what 'the Boss' would say." I had known for some years that while we had called Dr Frame "the Bishop," students would refer to me in my absence as "the Boss." Now, the cat was out of the bag and the title was to stick... at least, until replaced by "the Doc" some years later.

In another incident during that term at Beech Lawn a new student volunteered to do the laundry, for several of his delighted fellows, in the hot water boiler. Their delight turned to horror when white sheets, white shirts, etc., all came out a lovely rosy pink. Boiling red socks with the whites was not, apparently, an idea which recommended itself! On another occasion, Revd T.C. Mitchell, then pastor at Bolton First Church, in the course of one lecture on pastoral theology, stated that by the law of averages fifty percent of the class would not make it into the ministry. At the student prayer meeting one student, now a leading elder, told the Lord that "...they were not interested in the law of averages, but the law of assurance!"

In early October a local doctor from Ashton-under-Lyne became interested in buying Beech Lawn and made an offer which was close to the asking price. Details of the sale were completed before the students left for the Christmas break in December, but there was no sign of a new property on the horizon. We were a college without a location, a home without a house to put it in, a soul without a body.

Thus when Beech Lawn was sold it was with mixed feelings that we began to plan for the next stage of our journey. We were still not in sight of the promised land and one major question was: where will we store our furniture, especially the books? It was therefore a great relief when Dr Herd, the new owner of Beech Lawn, allowed us to keep the small house, to the rear of the main building, for one year. He had been a friend of Revd Peter Ferguson in former days and he refused any remuneration from us. We housed the six girls in the flat and thus cared for them, and the books were stored upstairs with the furniture, but what could we do for the men and for the Principal's family? The solution was for us to board out the men in the homes of our Ashton members, who graciously made them available.

At this time Revd and Mrs Maynard James were to be in Africa for six months and they generously made their home in Oldham available to us. Our son, Peter, was only days old when Beech Lawn was sold and less than a month old when we moved to Oldham.

We were a college in transit. Each morning I would drive our daughter Marjory to school in Stalybridge, collect the six girls from Beech Lawn and take them to the church hall in Ashton where we held our classes. We all ate lunch together in a local restaurant, then, when classes were over, I would take the girls back to Beech Lawn, do a little office work, collect Marjory from school and travel back to Oldham.

When we began this arrangement we were not aware that the solution to our need was on the way. Classes functioned fairly well and the pressures were not as great as they might have been. Life was hectic and we were trying to be as much a community as possible. There followed a testing time, one in which the character of the student body was to emerge strengthened. It was a period which made the eventual move even more satisfying.

One Sunday, two weeks into the term, I was due to preach in our Carmoor Road Church in Manchester. I left in good time and was making my way by car to the appointment. On this occasion (contrary to the habits of a lifetime!) I was travelling through the city at 25 miles per hour. Suddenly, at a crossroads, a car came through a stop sign, striking my car door. I was thrown clear, stunned but picked myself up and in a moment of reflex reaction bent into the car and switched off the engine. A kindly couple hurried out and took me into their shop. I was alert enough to give them the number of my telephone (installed three days earlier). Then, as I started to drink a cup of tea, I must have passed out. In the meantime, Nan was about to leave to walk to church with Marjory and Peter (who was only six weeks old) when the telephone rang. In a hurry, she was about to leave the phone unanswered, but finally picked it up and learned that I was in hospital.

Here we were in a new house, knowing no neighbours, with the hospital several miles away. The couple also called the home of Jack Ford, and Mrs Ford took the news to the church where they prayed for us in the morning service. One of the men, dear brother James Taylor, arranged for my car - a total wreck - to be moved. Nan finally came to the hospital and says I talked rationally (whatever that is) but I have no recollection of that visit. With two stitches in my forehead I was allowed home. Jack Ford came with his car to take me home, invited me to drive, and I did. I have always had a bit of a big head but it was considerably larger by next morning. God had surely given us His protection: three days later I was able to continue the daily routine.

A call from our estate agent, suggesting that he thought he had a property which we might like to view, found me driving to Didsbury and The White House. While we had been in residence at Beech Lawn we had made an offer for a lovely property known as Forest Edge out in Bowden, Cheshire. Our offer had been accepted but finally the owner withdrew the property from the market. Many of us (including General Superintendent Dr Hugh C. Benner) had set our hearts on "Forest Edge". The house had 20 acres of ground and was set in one of the lovely parts of Cheshire. We would never find a place like it; it had truly won our hearts. But as I walked up the avenue of The White House on a cold January day, I was pleasantly surprised at the beauty of the building, On entering the house with its lovely oak panelling, I was captivated and felt that this was surely God's provision for us.

The main building and outhouses had been built in 1914 and the materials used were of the best. The leaded windows built into thick oak window frames were impressive and the whole had an appearance of grandeur. It was owned by the Godlee family. Philip Godlee, who had been in textiles, had died, and the family home was being broken up. The house had a large music room, used by the Godlee family who performed as a string quartet. Philip Godlee had been chairman of the world famous Hallé Orchestra. They were keen that we should buy the property since they sensed we would preserve it intact. Eventually an offer of £9,500 was made and, by word of mouth, was accepted by the trustees selling the property. All seemed to be going well when suddenly we were informed that another offer, a little higher, had been made. We all felt that we should not start haggling. We had offered our final figure, it had been accepted, and we felt that any offers from other buyers should be turned down. That, indeed, was finally what happened.

However, we were not yet sure that we would be allowed to use the building as a theological college. We had decided to buy and hoped that the permission for change of use would be given. When Mr David Hopkins of Scatcherd Hopkins, Solicitors, proceeded to apply for permission he discovered that, because all the land was allocated, the original owners could not give permission, and we would be required to get signatures from all the neighbours stating that they had no objection to this change of use to a theological college. It was a discouraging thought. None of the neighbours knew who or what we were. Perhaps it was as well! Many of them followed a different religious persuasion and the situation could have been difficult.

Through the diligence of Mr David Hopkins, it was discovered that the land had belonged to two brothers, each of whom had sold their share. In the process there was one small (I mean small!) triangle of land, about one yard wide, tapering to nothing, which had not been sold. This enabled the members of the Ashley family, the original landowners, to grant the change of use and to sell us that scrap of land for £1. Surely God was working for us! Here we were, in an extremely fine residential district of Manchester, close to city facilities and with five acres of land for development! The move took place in April, 1959.

Photo No 22
The White House, Didsbury, Manchester

New direction   new challenge   83

Photo No 23
First Class of Students in The White House, 1959

The furniture and books which had been stored in the flat at Beech Lawn were moved in. The big question facing us concerned space: how we could possibly hope to house 20 students, a resident cook, and the Principal and his family in a house which contained a breakfast room (plus kitchen and pantries), seven bedrooms, and three public rooms?

The music room, which was the largest in the house, became the lecture room-cum-library. The morning room, which had a linking set of doors to the music room, became the general office. The other main room was the dining room. Sixteen of the students were housed in six of the bedrooms and the other four were housed in what had been a workshop attached to the washhouse and garage. The cook, Miss Lily Tuckley, was given the breakfast room off the kitchen as a bed-sitting room. We as a family were housed in one large bedroom, which had its own bathroom and a small dressing room where the children slept. Those were the housing arrangements for the first year.

Of course there were pressures and all kinds of experiments were thought up. Three of the students, John McGhee, Cyril Cutting and Ray Busby, were the handy men of the group. They installed extra plumbing and made an airing room into a bedroom. Rumour had it that I intended housing several students in the attic rooms, which some of the students protested were unhygienic! Student leaders came to protest; they threatened to inform the health authorities, and finally, in an act of protest, the majority of the students declared that they would not return. An appeal was made to the chairman of the Board, Dr Frame, but all to no avail. Finally it dawned on some, at least, that we as a family were suffering these conditions along with them and the objections were withdrawn. It was then revealed that the only people moving to the attic were our two children, who played and slept there over the next six years, and look back with some nostalgia on those days. Of course, it might have been better to have revealed to the protesters that this was the plan, but then my parents had been Irish, and some of their stubborn streak must have rubbed off on me!

Immediately after we moved into The White House, the Board of Governors began to plan for expansion. We had invested the entire proceeds from the sale of Hurlet and Beech Lawn in the purchase of the Didsbury property, so we immediately launched a fund-raising programme, ably assisted by Mr Len Shepherd, then a member of the Board. His professional ability as an artist and as a director of an advertising company were talents which he gave freely and fully to us. Plans were prepared for the building of a new dormitory and the remodelling of the garage wing of The White House. When completed in 1961 this gave us 21 study-bedrooms, a lecture room, and a common room. The total cost of this development, estimated at £14,000, was finally £18,000.

The General Church promised to match, pound for pound, the money raised on the Districts by June, 1960, up to £5,000. Our people made pledges and gifts and we set out to raise as much of the £5,000 as we could. I was at the 1960 General Assembly of the Church of the Nazarene when the final amount was raised. Thus we had more than half of the cost met prior to the dedication of the building.

The new building was called "Hurlet Hall" and the renovated garage wing "Beech Wing". Several churches and individuals sponsored rooms and paid for the furnishing of these, and these special gifts were recognised by the placing of the name of the donor above the door of the room.

We were further assisted by others who donated their labour. My father, in the final months of his life, built twenty-one beds: these were transported and assembled, and are still in use. Others made similar sacrificial gifts. In the summer of 1961, Dr G. B. Williamson officially dedicated the buildings and we were on course for development and growth.

Photo No 24
Dr G. B. Williamson, General Superintendent,
officially opening Hurlet Hall and Beech Wing, 1961

Photo No 25
Hurlet Hall, 1961

Housing, for staff, was another major concern. Alex and Joyce Deasley now lived in one half of what was the Dean's flat and we lived in the other half. Noise was difficult to contain, especially since our children were above the flats in the attics. We were then joined by Dr and Mrs Ford and their daughter Pauline, who lived across from the Deasley family. For six years we continued the routine and work of the college and it seemed that we were set to go on as a team for at least another decade.

We three were paid a total of £750 per year between us. In addition, we had room and board provided for us and our families. Space was at a minimum and the pressures were at times considerable; nevertheless, the strong relationships established between us were to be maintained over the years.

In 1964 a decision was taken by the General Church of the Nazarene - without any consultation with the college authorities in Britain - to establish a Bible college in Europe to prepare young people on the continent for ministry in the church. Although there was no obligation to consult British Nazarenes, the fact that this college, situated in Büsingen, Germany, was to carry out its instruction in English made the lack of communication very evident. This event made me very unsettled. Here in Britain, a college established some 20 years, labouring under staggering financial demands but well situated to teach students from the continent, was left to struggle on while the church spent thousands of dollars (millions, in the longer run) to establish an English-speaking college where the students were surrounded by a German-speaking population.

It seemed to us that the advantages of being in an English environment would have given European students greater facility in language study, exposed them to a wealth of library material, and developed cultural understanding between the nations of Europe and Britain. This state of affairs led me to give serious consideration to my own role in the European context and to conclude that the possibility for growth in the work of education in Britain was being seriously handicapped.

The pressure of the years had been considerable, and this new decision led me to consider resignation. For two years I struggled with the matter. I had been happy in my work and I had visions for growth; Jack Ford and Alex Deasley were magnificent colleagues in every way, our children were well settled in school, and the prospect of leaving all this was devastating. Wrestling month after month with the import of such a decision made me weary and frustrated. Finally, I asked God for clear guidance on the matter and in a remarkable way that guidance came. In September, 1965, I presented my twelfth annual report as Principal to the Board of College Trustees. Prior to taking my seat I asked for the indulgence of the chair and announced that as of June, 1966, I was resigning my office. I had struggled for many months with the decision, but had felt unable to share my struggle with anyone other than my wife.

The announcement came as a great surprise to all. Every opportunity was given to me to take time away and rest. Finally in December, at a special meeting of the Board of Trustees, my resignation was accepted. This ended a fourteen year association with the college which had been a very wonderful and exciting experience.

Now the college would move into a new era under the leadership of a new Principal. After deliberation, the Board decided to invite Revd Jack Ford to assume the leadership. After prayer and discussion he accepted the invitation.

By the close of the second decade in the life of the college, considerable stability had been achieved and the support of the first principal, George Frame, now the chairman of the Board of Trustees, was such that we were secure in the loyalty of the Board and the church.

A transition had been successfully made in leadership, the development of the new campus in Manchester was well underway and the uniting of Hurlet Nazarene College and Beech Lawn Bible College had taken place with comparative ease. British Isles Nazarene College was on its way. If the change in leadership was relatively easy, it was in large part as a result of the support given by Dr Frame and his outstanding colleagues on the Board of Trustees. Now it was time to move on and hand the reins of leadership to another. The future would reveal the strength of the foundation upon which we had built.

Photo No 26

Chapel Service in College Library, 1962

New direction new challenge 89

Photo No 27
Student Body, 1963

Photo No 28
Students and Lecturers, 1966

Chapter 9

A NEW HAND AT THE HELM

Jack Ford was a man whose influence was felt far beyond the confines of the Holiness Movement in which he was a leader for half a century. He was born in Hull, England, in 1908, in a comfortable, middle class home.

The son of a Hull business man who retired on his capital at the age of fifty-five, he attended Hymers College as a fee-paying pupil. He left school at the age of fifteen and a half and took life leisurely as a junior clerk in a corn merchant's office. A contact with a zealous tract distributor in the summer of 1927 stimulated a desire in him for a conscious relationship with God and an assurance of personal salvation.[26]

His conversion came after a time of private prayer. He had been brought up and confirmed in the Anglican Church but soon became involved with the International Holiness Mission in Coltman Street, Hull. It was here he learned about the experience of entire sanctification and, at a convention held by the Japan Evangelistic Band at Swanwick, Derbyshire, in June, 1928, he claimed the experience that was to transform his life and lead him into full-time ministry.

His close and long-standing friendship with Maynard James began when James went to Hull with the trekkers, young men who would travel from village to village to preach the gospel, carrying their mission tent and personal goods in a cart. They invited Ford to join them, which he did. Then in September, 1929, he entered Cliff College, the Methodist college for evangelists, serving as student chairman in his final term.

After spending the summer of 1930 leading a trekking party for the International Holiness Mission, Ford, still only twenty-two, was appointed to assist Leonard Wain at the headquarters of the mission in Battersea, London. After a six-month period in Battersea, he was appointed to the pastorate of the Addiscombe Mission Church in Croydon.

For the next three years he served as pastor until, in 1934, he left to join Maynard James and Michael Keeley on what became known as the "revival party." The development of this evangelistic thrust was very successful and had the initial blessing of the I.H.M. Executive Council.

Great advance was made in tent-campaigning, and this resulted in International Holiness Mission churches like Queensbury, Dewsbury and Keighley being established. It was during this year of significant advance and growth that men like James and Ford began to question the leadership of the International Holiness Mission. Jack Ford later wrote:

1934, the year of the greatest advance, was a year of contention and division. It closed with the International Holiness Mission bereft of its revival party and two of its new churches Salford and Oldham. [27]

The young evangelists left the I.H.M. to work independently and during the next five years the new movement, known as the Calvary Holiness Church, saw considerable growth and consolidation. Ford was at the side of his friend and colleague Maynard James, and during these years he served as secretary to the movement. Jack Ford's keen insight and preaching ability were to make him possibly the most influential man within the new movement. Maynard James had the charisma and the eloquence of an evangelist, in which role he excelled. The oldest of the four men who together founded the Calvary Holiness Church, James had been involved in the work of evangelism and also served as pastor for the International Holiness Mission in Manchester. In that pastorate he followed the outstanding preacher and Bible scholar, Revd Harry E. Jessop. James was the obvious choice to be President of the new movement. The other three, Ford, Filer and Ravenhill, all recognised his leadership talents.

But Jack Ford brought many qualities to the movement. As a pastor, teacher and preacher he spent his life in dedicated service to God and the church. One of Jack Ford's impressive characteristics was his utter dedication to the development of his spiritual life. I came across a diary which he had been using for his preaching engagements and other items of interest. The item which caught my attention was a very simple statement: "I had a gracious time of fellowship with the Lord this morning." It seemed to me that captured the central thrust of this good man's life. Whatever task he set himself to do, whatever role he was called upon to fill, however many talents he possessed - and he possessed many - at the very heart of his living was his relationship with God. A student of that time writes:

I remember Dr Ford most for his graciousness and winsomeness. The ordinary members of the church loved him dearly - this was obvious when on college "weekends" with him. I remember once visiting with him on the Brooklands, Manchester estate, when a lady just stopped him on the street to tell him her troubles. (He had on his dog collar).[28]

Clearly, his walk and communion with God were central to his life. Prayer for him was not a duty to be performed, but a daily expression of his love for God and of the fact that, for him, communion with God was more important than conversation with others. He was a conversationalist and a rare debater but he was first and foremost a man who had committed his life into the hands of God. There were those who felt that he was too holy to be real. The fact is that he *was* real even if this sometimes put him at odds with those with a more pragmatic approach to their faith.

The pastorates he held in Croydon, Gillingham, Sheffield and Ashton-under-Lyne all testify to the quality of a preaching ministry and the concern of a pastoral heart for the people to whom he ministered. Jack had an outstanding preaching gift. His mind was clear in his understanding of the great Biblical truths and his ability in communicating these truths was recognised by his colleagues and peers. Constantly in demand as a convention preacher he was also at home in the role of evangelist and made full proof of his ministry by being instrumental in pointing many to Christ. Letters which I have received in recent days from some of his former students indicate that while they were in college they wanted to model their ministry on men like Jack Ford.

It was while he was engaged in the busy pastorate in Sheffield that he studied for his Bachelor of Divinity degree with the University of London. This was no small achievement as he was also carrying responsibility for his church and playing a full part in the life of his denomination.

Although, he was late in coming to academic work the honours BD course gave him the opportunity to decide about future academic achievement. His interest was in Church History and it was to this subject that he turned for his doctoral work at the University of London. In addition, his interest turned to an analysis of the Holiness Movement as it followed in the footsteps of John Wesley. This became the focus of his research. Again, Jack embarked on no easy task. He was serving in a busy, demanding pastorate in Ashton when much of his research was done. In 1961 he joined the teaching staff of British Isles Nazarene College and endeavoured to complete his thesis.

The University of London took the unusual step of allowing him to have Professor Gordon Rupp of Manchester University as his supervisor, rather than insisting that one of London

University's professors be his adviser. It was a long road on which he embarked, but in 1967 the University of London awarded him his degree of Doctor of Philosophy. He was the first minister of the Calvary Holiness Church to graduate with his BD, and now had the honour of being the first British Nazarene minister to earn a PhD from a British university.

Photo No 29
Revd Dr Jack Ford, Principal, 1966-73

In 1960 Ford had been invited to join Rae and Deasley on the staff. This trio was dubbed "the three wise men of BINC."

Photo No 30
"The three wise men of BINC"

When the Fords came on campus, Mrs Ford undertook to teach English to the students who had no qualifications in that subject. Revd John Paton in a letter concerning his time in college says, "I really must not overlook Mrs Ford who spent many hours doing her very best to get me to speak...clearly enough to be understood."[29] As was the case with other members of staff we got two for the price of one.

In 1966 when I resigned from the college the Board of Governors elected Jack Ford as Principal. It would certainly have been to his advantage had the change-over been delayed for one more year. He was getting near the end of his doctoral thesis. Thus being appointed to the principalship of the college made it more difficult for him to complete his work.

Jack Ford was no stranger to the office of Principal. He had given four years to that office at Beech Lawn Bible College. The future of the work would benefit from his experience. Revd A. R. G. Deasley was to continue as a tutor with added responsibility as Dean. Jack Ford invited Revd Joe Reid to come to care for the residence facilities, which included responsibility for the kitchen and dining room needs. All seemed set for the growth of the college. It seemed that these changes would ease the burden. However, the delegation of responsibility became problematic and tensions emerged.

The indebtedness on the new dormitories was £4,000, the total cost having been £18,000. Resources were very limited and the repayment of this loan would not be easy in the economic climate of the late sixties, however, 1966 saw a full body of students and the prospects were good.

The second half of the 1960s was the period of student unrest around the world. The old values, the accepted disciplines of the past, were being challenged on every hand. It was not possible for a Christian college not to be affected. Indeed, other Nazarene colleges in the United States and Canada were affected and the authority of the administration challenged.

It would seem that a small college like ours would miss this turmoil, but at least two factors contributed to the unease and the decline of these years. Ford was completing his doctoral work and this put added pressure on him and others. In addition he clearly belonged to "the old school" which saw discipline in very black and white terms. The place of the student was that of obedient participant in the life of the college, under a kind of benevolent despotism. In earlier years that was much easier to implement. Now, the young people coming to college, many of whom had been in the work place, were accustomed to much more freedom in their decision making and in the ordering of their lives. This meant that the restrictions of college life produced severe friction.

There was, however, some good progress made in the academic field. Dr Ford had introduced courses which would enable students to sit the examinations leading to the Certificate of Religious Knowledge, offered through the University of London, and a number of students gained this certificate during these years.

At this time the balance of the indebtedness on Hurlet Hall was paid off and a new fund for further building was established. This was the beginning of the financial support which made possible in 1978 the building of the J. B. Maclagan Chapel and new dining hall and kitchen facilities.

Photo No 31
Students and Staff, Autumn, 1966

Other factors made the growth of the college difficult. In 1969 Alex Deasley resigned to continue his doctoral work at Manchester. Joe Reid had resigned after only one year. He had hoped to be involved in counselling students but the practical demands on him had been so heavy that this did not happen and he felt unable to continue. That was a severe loss since his concern for people was always an important part of his ministry.

In January, 1970, Revd Dr T. C. Mitchell, who had been teaching at European Nazarene Bible College, came to the college as a tutor. "T. C." had come under the influence of the preaching of Revd J. B. Maclagan in the late 1930s, when Maclagan had been pastor of Parkhead Church of the Nazarene. Coming from the Bethany Hall, a large evangelistic mission which had grown out of the Moody revivals of the previous century, Mitchell absorbed the Wesleyan teaching and became an authority on John and Charles Wesley. With a minimum of formal education, T. C., through intensive personal study, was to become an eminent teacher and scholar. He had taught classes as a visiting lecturer when he was a pastor in Paisley and again when the college moved to Manchester.

Dr Mitchell had pastored the Ilkeston, Paisley, Bolton, and Thomas Memorial (London) churches prior to accepting the invitation of his friend, Dr John Neilson, Rector of European Nazarene Bible College, to join the staff of ENBC. The resignation of Alex Deasley had seriously weakened the teaching staff of BINC, so when Ford invited T. C. to join him in Manchester there was a great sense of anticipation. T. C. was an excellent communicator, and students who sat under his ministry were never disappointed in either the content or the communication of the subject.

He taught at BINC from January 1970 until March 1976. During that time he and his wife contributed to the whole life of the college. His coming to BINC brought Jack Ford a well informed teacher and brought his students a wealth of knowledge. His great love was history, especially that which surrounded the Wesley brothers, John and Charles.

In 1971, Revd William Rolland with Lois, his wife, returned from the USA where Bill had graduated with his Master of Divinity degree from Nazarene Theological Seminary. Bill Rolland had grown up in the Church of the Nazarene in Dunfermline, Scotland. He was a five-year-old Sunday school scholar when I pastored the Dunfermline church, and had a mischievous twinkle in his eyes and an enchanting smile which was to captivate many who met him. His talent for promotional work was seen when, as a student, he produced a delightful brochure, celebrating twenty years in the life of the college. His leadership of trekking teams and his enthusiasm and vision for BINC were the hallmark of his years as a student.

Bill came to work on recruitment and Lois served as office secretary. As a result of his untiring efforts and enthusiasm, student enrolment began to increase and he laid a foundation upon which we were to build over the years. Lois had come to the college as a student in 1966. While there she and Bill met and were married. Lois had exceptional musical skill, and Bill and Lois developed a musical ministry in these years which was a tremendous success and which in many ways brought the college to the attention of a larger constituency. They gathered around them a group of students and young people who formed a musical group which travelled widely in Britain presenting to large audiences the Christian musical *Life,* bringing the college and the work of the Church of the Nazarene greater visibility.

Perhaps we were slow in recognising the value of this work and I would take this opportunity to place on record the debt which

British Nazarenes owe to Bill and Lois. They are held in great affection by many young people of that day and we know that many were influenced to consider full time Christian work because of them.

These three men, Ford, Mitchell and Rolland along with Miss Roberts, the redoubtable catering manager, were the full complement of staff when Dr Ford retired in 1973. Former students Malcolm and Joyce Dawson served as warden and purchasing manager. These all held the college together in what were difficult and impoverished days. They faced difficulties which most people would have been unwilling to accept, but each was strong in commitment to God and love of the college.

Photo No 32
Students and Staff, 1972-73

The college faced great financial privation through these years. Salaries were very low and it was impossible to make income meet expenditure, even though people were generous in their support of the work. The fact of the matter was that from such a small base, fewer than 5,000 British Nazarenes, it was impossible to continue to operate. The question confronting the Board of Governors was how to make the college a viable proposition - a question which still does not have a fully satisfactory answer.

Meanwhile, Dr Edward S. Mann had been elected to be Executive Secretary in the Department of Education in Kansas City. He was undoubtedly God's man for this time. Colleges such as those in Canada and the British Isles were in need of some outside support. Dr Mann visited these and other campuses and with insight began to devise plans which might help these institutions.

For twenty-eight years the college had been trying to function as an educational institution with totally inadequate funding. When Jack Ford assumed responsibility in 1966 the whole economic climate in Britain was clearly changing. Salaries and consequently costs were on the increase and by 1970 it was clear that his task was all but impossible. Both district assemblies were aware of the inadequate salaries being paid to college staff, a situation made worse by the fact that pastors were also inadequately paid.

The solution to this lay neither in the hands of the Board of Governors nor the District Assemblies. To grow, the college needed more students, but that required church growth; such growth in the church required that the programme of the college be developed to attract and prepare a larger number of people.

This was the state of things when Jack Ford came to the point of retirement. Our best efforts would be futile unless the whole philosophy of the place and purpose of the college was analysed. It was to this end that Edward Mann directed the attention of the Board of Governors. He realised that drastic measures were necessary and financial support from the General Church would be required.

Photo No 33
Trekking party, 1964
from L-R Robert Brown, Bill Rolland, Jim Martin and Gwyn Downing

A new hand at the helm 103

Photo No 34
Students and Staff, 1963

Photo No 35
Students on College Week-end with Revd John Weatherill

Photo No 36
Students and Staff, 1967-68

Photo No 37
Revd Dr Hugh Rae, Principal,
1954-66; 1973-86

Chapter 10

WHEN ENOUGH IS NOT ALLOWED TO BE ENOUGH

In 1971 Dr Ford indicated that he wished to retire as Principal as soon as a successor was found. This was seen as a time to re-evaluate the financial needs of the college, and matters were set in motion with the General Superintendent (Dr George Coulter) and the General Board. The Board of Governors met to elect a Principal and agreed to extend an invitation to Revd Dr Alex Deasley. He had just completed his doctoral thesis under the guidance of Professor F. F. Bruce, examining *The Idea of Perfection in the Dead Sea Scrolls*.

Dr Deasley gave the invitation serious consideration, and even decided to accept, but finally felt that would be for him a wrong decision, and instead went to Canadian Nazarene College as Professor of New Testament Studies. It is impossible to estimate the contribution which Alex and Joyce Deasley made to the college. In almost every letter from graduates of that time reference is made to the outstanding contribution which Alex Deasley made to their lives. His teaching ministry was challenging and stimulating. To this was added a pulpit ministry which in the mind of the writer has had no equal for its lucidity of thought and its anointing by the Spirit. This was one loss which the British church could ill afford and, while the General Church of the Nazarene benefited from his years at Nazarene Theological Seminary, the church in Britain was undoubtedly the poorer for his going. My association with Alex goes back before his student days at Hurlet and, over the years, my life has been enriched by his ministry and his friendship. He was to lay a foundation in Biblical Studies which more recent scholars have built upon. Both Alex and Joyce hold a very special place in the life of the college. He was a colleague for whom I hold the highest esteem: a scholar of exceptional ability, but above all a preacher of the Word and a true man of God.

The Board of Governors was now faced with the problem of finding someone else to assume the leadership of the college. After much discussion it was decided to ask Dr Frame to visit Winnipeg and discuss the possibility of my returning to Manchester for a second term as Principal. We had moved there in 1968 when I joined the staff of Canadian Nazarene College. It was a cold week-end when I met Dr Frame, who was already an ill man. This was to be his final act on behalf of the college board prior to his retirement at the District Assembly. We were honoured to have him come and share the concerns of the Board of Governors with us. We entertained Dr Frame in our home in Winnipeg and discussed the whole proposition.

As a family we were very happy in Winnipeg and the prospect of returning to Britain was not easy for us to consider. However, I had been telling Canadian Nazarenes that if CNC was to survive and make its contribution to the life of the church in Canada it would only be if Canadian Nazarenes, many of whom drifted to the more financially secure USA, were prepared to remain in Canada and serve the college and the church. As I was thinking and praying about the invitation to return to Manchester, the thought kept coming to me that the only way that the church in Britain would grow would be if British Nazarenes would remain there.

This was a dilemma indeed. Here we were, four years in Winnipeg, settled into our own home, enjoying what we were doing. Marjory, our daughter, was in university; I was doing post-graduate work at the University of Manitoba; Nan was working in the school system and enjoying being a teacher - aide; Peter was still in high school. Everything rational said, "Stay where you are." For several months I thought about the invitation. I discussed it with my family, all of whom were willing to be guided by how I felt. I talked it over with Dr Arnold Airhart, President of CNC, and with some of my colleagues. This was the hardest decision I have ever had to make and so for months I "halted between two opinions." In August, 1972 we travelled as a family to Kansas City to talk with Dr Coulter and Dr Mann about some of the financial matters which would affect my decision.

I had resigned in 1966 because of the pressure of small resources and the establishing of the college in Europe. Nothing had changed very much and I felt that unless the General Church made a commitment to Britain this was the time to admit that we could no longer support a college. These were my thoughts on the matter. Others, I am sure, felt the same, but few would admit to that. I was asking for long term support for the college. Assurance was given that the General Board of the Church of the Nazarene saw this as a new situation and would give support in the future. That is now twenty years ago, and it must go on record that in all these years the General Church, through the General Superintendents and the General Board, has not failed us.

I returned from Kansas City and informed the new chairman of the Board of Governors, Revd Thomas W. Schofield, that I would be willing to let my name be presented to the Board. What I did not tell him was that I had decided that if there were two or more negative votes, we would not consider coming. In the event there was one negative vote. We decided to return and the wheels began to move. I asked to meet the Board of Governors at Christmas and flew to Manchester for that purpose. I wanted to be certain that the programme which I felt should be implemented really had the support of this board. I was convinced that seeking affiliation with Canadian Nazarene College on the Bachelor of Theology degree programme would be a first step on the road to institutional accreditation. I felt convinced that we needed to offer our young people the best preparation we could and, looking back, I am convinced that this was a good decision.

It was clear to me that if we were to embark on this kind of educational programme we would need added teaching staff with strong academic qualifications. This view was not a judgment on those who were already teaching. My own academic background and preparation were limited. I was comfortable teaching History and Philosophy, but if we affiliated with CNC then we would need more teachers who were scholars in specialised fields. This would not happen overnight, but it needed to be in our vision for the future.

As I began to think about the future staffing of the college three things happened which encouraged me to believe that I was making the right decision in returning to Manchester. First there was a letter from Revd Herbert McGonigle, then pastoring in Leeds. In this letter, after welcoming us back to Britain, he expressed his long-time desire to teach at BINC and to do that under my leadership. He was at that time completing his BD degree with London University. I replied that I was sure there could be a place for him in the future, and advised him to continue towards an MA and perhaps a PhD. Knowing the size of the college and its resources, I often wonder how that reply struck him. That he continued along the road that finally brought these achievements to pass says much for his foresight and commitment.

The second event was a conversation which I had with Dr Edward Mann. He suggested that since we planned to affiliate with CNC, it would be good to get someone as Academic Dean who could lay a strong foundation. He suggested that Dr Harvey Blaney, long-time professor at Eastern Nazarene College in Quincy, Massachusetts, might be prepared to come for a few years.

Dr Blaney's acceptance of the invitation and his contribution to the academic programme was to be a factor of great importance in the future direction of the college. The Blaneys were to become a much-loved couple on the college campus and beyond. Dr Blaney brought a thoroughness to the foundational needs of the college which made future Academic Deans grateful for his ability, and his spirit was such that he was loved by us all and influenced us in many ways during the three years which he spent in Manchester.

The third event was a telephone call from a young Canadian farmer, a graduate of CNC and ENC, Kent Brower. Kent had come to CNC to teach a one-month winter term. It was a slack time on the farm in Alberta and he had been able to leave. Immediately we met we felt a common bond and he now wanted to know if there was any possibility of his teaching at BINC. I already had added Dr Blaney to the staff and had no real intention of taking another person on board. I still was not sure how we would finance what we had already planned and to add to that was not in my plan.

In addition, there was the question of how the British would take to another North American coming to teach. Nevertheless, I did not turn his request down out of hand, although I did not expect that we could have him. The idea was that Francine, his wife, would teach in the school system and that he would begin doctoral work at Manchester under Professor F. F. Bruce. I talked at length to Dr Deasley, who was then on staff at CNC. He felt certain that the possibility of Kent being accepted by F. F. Bruce was extremely remote. In addition, it would be difficult for Francine to get teaching permission. On this basis I called Kent and suggested that if Francine was given permission to teach and if he was accepted by Professor Bruce then we would take that as a sign for them to come.

I was certain that these conditions would not be fulfilled, and dismissed the matter. Several months passed and in April a call came from Kent to say that Francine would be allowed to teach and he had been accepted by F. F. Bruce. Now I was in trouble! I said that they should come and that I would work something out in the meantime. I had not, however, informed the Board of Governors about the possibility of this taking place.

I called Revd T. W. Schofield to tell him that this young couple were coming and that I was sure we could use them, would somehow house them, and give them a small part-time salary. That event was to be one of the most providential happenings in the life of the college. Kent and Francine were to become an integral part of the future of BINC in a manner that would not have seemed possible at the time. The fact is that the entire future of the college was set in motion as a result of these three events.

There was an air of excitement and anticipation as the new college year began that autumn of 1973. Returning students knew that there would be changes that would affect them in quite dramatic ways. The seven years which had elapsed since my resignation in 1966 had brought many changes to the college and to me as an individual. My years in Canada had made a tremendous impression on my thinking with regards to the mission of the college and the methods which would need to be employed if the vision of those days was to become a reality. The influence of Dr Arnold Airhart, President of Canadian Nazarene College, on my thinking was such that I wanted to emulate something of his spirit and bring some of the kind of vision which he had for Canada back to the British scene. The opportunity given to me to become a better teacher and the influences of colleagues in disciplines other than religion were all bringing about changes which for me were very meaningful and important. CNC was larger than BINC, but not too much so, and therefore administratively I learned a great deal from those years.

In setting in motion the Canadian ThB programme I had the advantage of having been involved in it for five years. Dr Blaney had been involved in the degree programmes of Eastern Nazarene College. Kent Brower was a graduate of CNC and had done work under Dr Blaney while at ENC. In addition to this, the men who were already on the staff were able to help us integrate the diploma and the degree courses.

A small college with a small staff is always pressed for time to get the administration as well oiled as it would like. That I knew from my previous years. The addition of two more staff members, who also assumed administrative responsibilities, meant that we were now for the first time able to develop the machinery which would make the whole task simpler and much more efficient. Much of the record keeping had been in the hands of Dr T.C. Mitchell and was, as one would expect, meticulously kept. As Dr Blaney began to integrate the whole of the academic programme he was ably assisted by Dr Mitchell.

Revd. Dr Bill Rolland, as he was to become, was excited about the prospects of growth and spearheaded all kinds of promotional programmes which bore much needed fruit in those early days of the 70s. This would yield a good harvest through the seventies, and we were sorry in 1978 when Bill felt that it was time to move on.

Kent Brower took over the role of Bursar. That was an area which was very important and one which I had previously undertaken. I became aware of the fact that Kent was an assiduous worker in all that he undertook, and very quickly the finances of the college improved. During the next thirteen years we were able to operate every year in the black. It was, of course, made easier by the fact that we had a basic budget allocated from the General Church and also by the fact that our churches took upon themselves increased budgets, and that payment of these was always a priority.

Thus the college of the 1970s was vastly different in its management from the college of the previous three decades. The future was full of challenge and the new direction was one which would create an institution which was set to fulfil the ideals set by its founding principal, Dr George Frame. He had chosen as the motto "Scholarship on Fire," and the emphasis on high spirituality plus first class academic preparation was the ideal to be striven for at all times.

How successful the combination of scholarship and spirituality has been must be for history to judge, but it has, I know, always been central to the understanding of all who have had a part in the ministry of the college over the decades.

Photo No 38
Students and Staff, 1974

Chapter 11

VISION AND ITS COST

Without doubt, 1973 was a watershed in the life of the college. It was one thing for the Board of Governors to commit themselves to a new approach to training, but another matter to ride the inevitable storms that such a process would create. Until 1972 the college had adopted a "training" orientation: now it was attempting to bring discipline to the minds of students, to lay a basis on which they could build a growing edge to their ministry. Practics was an essential part of that—but Practics without exegetical equipment and theological understanding was no longer sufficient for the ministry to which the church was called in the last quarter of the century.

We were to face criticism and suspicion, and encounter open antagonism to some essential changes. Some of the criticism was unjust and unexpected, but by and large it grew out of a misunderstanding of the objectives. It had been the practice to judge the success or failure of the college according to the number of graduates entering and remaining in the ministry. This was a natural form of judgment, but only valid when it took into account the many factors outwith the college. This point was well expressed in the words of Dr Tom Noble, in his observation that the college is not a source but a channel. The college alone cannot call people to the ministry, that must happen mainly at the grass roots, which is the local church.

It was thus with excitement and apprehension that we set out to have informal discussions with our constituents throughout Britain. Dr Edward Mann, who had been so supportive during our months of indecision, had arranged to be in Britain during September and October of 1973. He and I had planned a series of rallies in various parts of the country, where we met ministers and lay people in open forum, and began to articulate our vision for the development of the work of the college and, in particular, the proposals which would lead to our students earning the Bachelor of Theology degree through Canadian Nazarene College. We engaged in discussion with our people as to the role of the college in Britain and, from, these discussions, gathered a considerable dossier of ideas and hopes. Some expressed their fears that a Canadian degree would not be accepted in British circles. Those fears we readily understood, and recognised that this was an obstacle. However, we hastened to point out that only students who had the entrance qualifications for a British university would be admitted to the degree. This meant that we would preserve the high standard which we deemed essential. It also encouraged students to get these qualifications prior to coming to college or, in some instances, in the first years of their attendance at BINC.

Fears were expressed (both inside and outside the college) that we would lose sight of our central purpose, and that in the long run the church would suffer. We pondered this and tried to develop over the next ten years a curriculum strategy which would avoid as many of these pitfalls as possible. Perhaps the most encouraging thing to come out of these *ad hoc* discussions was a growing sense of support on the part of our people a feeling of anticipation in the air, as the college renewed its vision.

Dr Blaney set to work on the development of the curriculum and by 1976 our first two ThB students, Susan B. Raddings and Brian Davies, successfully graduated. Within four years Susan was teaching in a Manchester school - the first of many to find the value of the ThB.

Student enrolment increased steadily, and when the "30 barrier" was broken we felt we were on the way to real growth. Some had suggested that 30 students were as many as we could reasonably expect from such a small recruitment base, but programmes were devised and developed to recruit young people who were not expressly called to the full-time preaching ministry. Again, this move was questioned, and we responded by affirming that where the church has young people, it also has a definite obligation to give them the best opportunities to develop at every level. And of course, many who came to college in this way finally found a place of service in the full-time ministry of the church.

New programmes for lay training were devised and Bill Rolland recruited with greater fervour than ever. Young people were encouraged to enrol in the college and there was great excitement. Students from America had been coming in increased numbers and we faced the possibility of an invasion! However, the problem never became a real one, since increasing numbers of students from within Britain made the percentage smaller than had been feared.

Growth brings its own demands and challenges. A larger student body meant pressure on facilities. More married students applied, and some had children. Where were they to be housed? At first they found their own accommodation near the college, but this grew more difficult to find. Some were able to purchase property in Manchester, but in the end we knew that we would need to acquire housing off campus. The present buildings on campus were getting much too cramped. The dining room, located in The White House, was rapidly becoming too small for our regular needs, let alone any special occasions like Christmas or graduation banquets. Growth in numbers also meant increasing staff, and that in turn meant additional financing and housing. How could we meet these demands?

In March, 1976, after six years of diligent service at BINC, Dr T. C. Mitchell accepted an appointment on the staff of Nazarene

Bible College, Colorado Springs. As a teacher he had been greatly loved; as a preacher much in demand; and as a colleague greatly respected for the thoroughness of his preparation and the incisiveness of his mind. His going broke a link with the past. Then, in July of 1976, Dr Harvey Blaney returned to the United States. His three-year contract completed, he and his wife felt that they should return home. Mrs Blaney had been an inspiration to us all. Despite ill health, she had taken some part in the activities of the college and had been involved regularly in the meetings of student wives which my wife had started soon after our return to Britain. Dr Blaney had made a unique contribution to the college and laid foundations upon which others were to build. His enthusiastic spirit and quiet optimism had helped us overcome early difficulties and gave to his successors goals towards which they would move in the coming years.

The going of these much-respected staff members presented the Board of Governors with important decisions. Dr Blaney's successor clearly needed to be someone who could grasp the significance of his vision and apply it to the British culture. Our affiliation to CNC was such that we had liberty to adjust the programme within certain parameters, and we needed an Academic Dean who could do that. There were clearly two front runners.

The first, Kent Brower, had been a full-time staff member since 1974, and had been serving as Bursar. He had been to finances what Harvey Blaney had been to curriculum during the years from 1973. In addition, he was a graduate of Canadian Nazarene College and was familiar with the ThB programme. The other was Thomas A. Noble, at that time completing his Bachelor of Divinity degree at the University of Edinburgh. He had been elected a member of the Board of Governors in 1972 in succession to his father and was a graduate of two British universities, Glasgow and Edinburgh.

Several factors reinforced my final decision to present T. A. Noble's name to the Board in 1976. He was a familiar figure in the North British Isles District and had earned the respect of his peers as well as that of his elders. He also shared my feelings about the need to re-evaluate the whole approach of the British church to the question of ministry and the preparation for it.

To summarise, since returning from Canada in 1973, it had become a matter of growing concern to me that the college, after thirty years, was still faced with the dilemma of a two tier system of ministerial preparation. On the one hand, we encouraged young people to enrol as students at the college to prepare for our ministry. On the other hand, men and women would come to District Superintendents (who were chronically short of pastors) and, on applying for the ministry, would be given a church and placed on a home study course. It seemed that a young person who had grown up in the Church of the Nazarene and felt called to enter the ministry was likely to be directed to the college, however, a person who came from another denomination who applied to the ministry, especially married applicants, would immediately be given a church to pastor! This seemed to me to be an unacceptable approach. Those who knew the church and its teaching best were asked to spend three years in college, while those who were total strangers to the denomination were put in charge of a congregation.

After much thought and prayer I suggested to the Board of Governors that they request that the Executive Council (the joint Advisory Boards) set up a Commission on the Ministry and the College. Their brief was to study the whole question of entrance to and preparation for the ministry. Members elected to this Commission were drawn from both districts, and included leading elders and laymen. Revd Leslie Evans was appointed chairman and T. A. Noble (as yet a governor) was elected secretary. The two District Superintendents

(Revd D. J. Tarrant and Revd T. W. Schofield) and the college Principal were included on the commission. Several meetings were held and a final printed report was presented to both District Assemblies for their approval.

The report was approved, and, in 1976, was passed by both District Assemblies and implemented. In effect, it meant that all those coming into the Nazarene ministry would spend at least the equivalent of one year at the college. An annual selection conference would be held to which all applicants to the ministry would be invited. The selection panel would include two elders from each District (elected from the Board of Ministerial Credentials), one layman from each district, the District Superintendents, the college Principal, and one other member of the college staff. T. A. Noble was elected secretary, an office which he has continued to hold. His coming to the college as Academic Dean later that year facilitated the execution of the proposals made by the Commission.

In the course of the meetings of the Board of Governors held in February, 1976, the question of replacing Mitchell and Blaney was high on the priority list. Tom Noble came to my office to talk with me about the replacement for Dr Blaney, and suggested that Kent Brower would be a good choice. Looking across my desk at him I agreed that Kent would have the qualifications for the work, but that I would opt for Tom himself, if he were willing to consider joining the staff. In the end, the Board of Governors invited Tom to become Academic Dean, an offer he accepted. If 1973 saw one watershed, then this was another. Tom and Elaine Noble and their family have in the past eighteen years proved pivotal to the development of the college, and that decision of the Board of Governors, though difficult, proved timely indeed.

At that same meeting of the Board of Governors, Revd Herbert McGonigle was invited to join the staff to replace Dr T. C. Mitchell. Herbert had come to Hurlet Nazarene College as a student in 1957. He had been introduced to the Church of the

Nazarene in Enniskillen when he met Revd J. B. Maclagan. He had been thinking of the ministry, and when J. B. talked to him about the college, he came to study. After serving pastorates in Walthamstow and Uddingston he came to the Dewsbury Road congregation in Leeds. A keen Wesley scholar, he joined the staff, and moved to Manchester with his wife Jeanne and their two sons, Stephen and Jonathan.

Housing the staff was now a matter of some concern, since resources were limited. When we purchased our own home the McGonigles moved into the college house in Albemarle Avenue. The Noble family also purchased their own home, and housing allowances were given to those who were buying. The Brower family, who had been in an apartment off campus, now moved into the flat in the college which had been the home of the Mitchells. Kent now added to his work by assuming the role of Dean of Students, with responsibility for campus life.

Other staff had been added. In 1973, Miss Roberts was serving as catering manager, and Lois Rolland as secretary. In 1974, Karen Ehrlen came to work in the office and to act as Dean of Women. In 1975, Norma Wilson, a graduate of BINC and the Nazarene Seminary in Kansas City joined the staff as Dean of Women, librarian, secretary, and teacher, roles which she filled with great success until she and her husband, Andrew Downie, moved to Edinburgh in 1984. Norma transformed the library, and encouraged churches and individuals to send historical material to create college archives. Ever a willing worker, Norma contributed to the whole life of the college in a manner that influenced and encouraged many of the students. We seemed set for growth and the decade of the 70s was certainly one which rang the changes in every area of college life. The question of housing and other facilities was, however, still a pressing one.

Revd J. B. Maclagan had been the District Superintendent on the British Isles South District from its beginnings in 1953. During the fourteen years of his leadership many changes had been made and his influence had been a very significant factor in the development of the college. Soon after J.B.'s death in 1967, Dr Ford presented proposals to the Board of Governors on future plans for the college. New residences for students were envisaged and it was proposed that fundraising begin. Further, the project was to include a chapel dedicated to the memory of James Baxter Maclagan. These proved to be years of decline in student numbers and in resources; nevertheless, some financial support had been given to the proposal.

In 1975 the project was revived and a young architect, Michael Hulme, was invited by the Board of Governors to prepare plans for a chapel with teaching unit. Michael had been interested in the college for several years and, indeed, his thesis for his degree had focused on the design of a theological college. His imaginative ability produced a design for a chapel and dining complex which excited us all, and in 1978 the Maclagan Chapel and new dining facility was opened officially by Mrs Jean B. Maclagan, with the dedication address given by Dr Edward Mann, Director of Nazarene Education, who had been a keen promoter of the plan. This simple but beautiful chapel was a fitting memorial to a man whose love for order and beauty in worship was legendary. It was to become the centre of campus life and, over the sixteen years since its opening, has served the interests of the college and community.

Photo No 39
J.B. Maclagan Chapel

Photo No 40
New Dining Hall adjoining the Chapel

Photo No 41
Unveiling of Plaque by Mrs Jean B Maclagan,
Revd Dr David Maclagan and Revd Dr Hugh Rae

Photo No 42
Dr Edward Mann giving dedication address, 1978

The removal of dining facilities from the main White House building enabled us to develop new offices and teaching facilities. One General Superintendent had been heard to remark on a visit, "You must get that cooking odour out of this administration building." I am sure that others of his colleagues might well have agreed with the sentiments of this English-born Canadian. Whatever the results in that respect, the ensuing development of the administrative and teaching facilities was significant.

Prior to the building of the chapel, housing for staff became an urgent need. When Bill and Lois Rolland joined the staff they were asked to share accommodation with another staff member. The facilities were somewhat improved for them after 1973, but the need for student housing, plus the need to have staff live off campus, was pressing. In the summer of 1974, property at 83 Dene Road came on the market, a three bedroom semi-detached house within a two minute walk of the college. The purchase price of £9,500 was offered and accepted. A neighbour and college friend gave us a bridging loan of £9,000 to enable us to make the purchase and to allow time to arrange for necessary mortgage requirements. This property has been in constant use for more than twenty years and has been a valuable asset to the college.

The purchase allowed the Rolland family to move off campus, and at the same time released very valuable college accommodation for the growing student intake. The Department of Home Missions under the direction of Dr Raymond Hurn gave the college a $15,000 loan towards the purchase, with the understanding that if we repaid the loan within a three year period we would only be required to repay $12,000. Needless to say, that kind of incentive made the repayment essential and we met the deadline with months to spare. Each added piece of property made the institution more secure, yet also added to the cost of maintaining the physical plant.

Increased property meant increased rates and running costs, but the growth of student numbers and the continued support of our people made possible the development of the next ten years. The question of accommodation for married students was now pressing. Until 1979 it had been relatively easy for couples to find accommodation at a reasonable price, but as house prices rose, so rental costs increased, and we decided to seek to purchase at least one property for conversion into self-contained flats. By 1980 Eleanor Brocklebank had become Administrative Assistant, and on her shoulders much of this responsibility fell.

We looked at some large houses, but the prices being asked seemed excessive, particularly when most of them needed considerable modernisation. A large property came on the market at the end of Lancaster Road. This, we felt, would serve several functions, and would have given some eight separate one-bedroom apartments. We placed a bid of £110,000, but another buyer was prepared to pay more and we felt that we had offered all that we dare. Finally, in 1982 a property came on the market, located on Clothorn Road, north of the college in Didsbury village, and we purchased this for £49,000. It offered the prospect of four self-contained, one-bedroom apartments, but needed £30,000 - £40,000 spent on it to bring it up to the required standard. We had hoped to get local government assistance for the work, but discovered that the government was withdrawing from the programme. However, we were finally able to carry through the renovations, with 80% of the building cost carried by the local authority, and our mortgage was structured so as to be financed through rental payments from the four dwellings.

When another property came on the market in 1984 in Clyde Road, West Didsbury, we purchased it for £25,000. It, too, required considerable work to be fully fit for family habitation. Ultimately, the task proved too onerous, and the demand for married housing diminished, so the building was sold, and, thanks to changes in the housing market, the college realised a profit which helped ease other financial pressures. These strategic moves were made possible through the vision and effort of the Administrative Assistant, whose diligence in finding funding and trimming expenditure were legendary.

However, we still were paying almost £400 per month to the department of Home Missions on the loan for the chapel and dining facilities. Some £12,000 was still outstanding on this loan when the Department of World Missions (from the Alabaster Fund) decided to pay out the entire indebtedness, which meant that by the mid-eighties we were free of debt (apart from the payments on 10, Clothorn Road, which were actually self-financing). We were again assisted by a further gift of $50,000 from the General Church.

Thus when our neighbour, Major Ralph Raffles, decided to place Dene House on the market we were able to purchase this at a cost of £140,000. The financing of this strained the resources of the college, but the additional library, housing and office facilities have been essential and, as I shall show in the next chapter, made future academic developments possible.

The refurbishing of Dene House was to be a mammoth task and the manner in which it was accomplished has certainly made excellent use of these facilities. Revd Walter Crow, then Rector of European Nazarene College, Büsingen, Germany, came to Manchester and set in motion the building of shelving essential to the housing of the many volumes. John Edgar (the maintenance supervisor) took over the major responsibility of this work and when it was completed Dene House became a focal point for students. The facility is delightfully designed and as I write it is evident that the accommodation is already almost too small.

In 1985 I had indicated to the Board of Governors that I planned to retire in July of 1986. This would bring to an end my service to the college. For twenty seven years I had had the privilege of being part of the training arm of the Church of the Nazarene.

At the annual meeting held in February, 1986 the Board elected Revd Herbert McGonigle as my successor. For nine years he had been a full time member of staff. His appointment was significant in that he represented a younger generation of scholars and they were set to lead the college into the 90s. As we will recount in the following chapter that leadership was to bring exciting changes to the college. The purchase of Dene House while adding financial pressure, was a major asset in the plans now unfolding in the life of the college. Over the next four years the academic breakthrough would come. To this development we must now turn our attention.

Photo No 43
Revd Dr Herbert McGonigle, Principal, 1986 -

Photo No 44
Revd Dr Eugene Stowe and Revd Herbert McGonigle
at the dedication of new Library, 1987

Chapter 12

A VISION REALISED

It was a wintry afternoon in January, 1990, and I sat in my office at Canadian Nazarene College in Winnipeg with the outside temperature below minus 20°C. To that point it had been another good if ordinary day, and I was back at CNC in what was euphemistically called my "retirement". Suddenly the day was changed utterly, and the ordinary gave way to the extraordinary. The general office called me on the telephone to say that I had a long distance call from Manchester. Answering the phone I heard the voice of Herbert McGonigle. I caught a note of excitement as he informed me that the college had been unanimously approved by the Council for National Academic Awards (CNAA) to grant the BA degree. I felt honoured that he should have taken the time to call me and let me know first hand this development. It would be difficult to find words that would adequately express my feelings. It was a high moment indeed and one which the founder of the college, Dr Frame, would have relished and appreciated.

When I put the telephone down, I jumped up from my desk like an excited schoolboy who simply had to share his news. I knocked on an adjacent office door and when a voice called, "come in", I entered and in an excited voice said, "BINC has been granted accreditation." The occupant was my son, Peter, and he was thrilled to hear the news. I then rushed to the offices of other staff members, sharing with them this moment and savouring the full implication of it.

I reflected that CNC was the institution which in 1973 had granted us affiliation in the Bachelor of Theology programme and in a special way this success at BINC was their success as well. As we later sat in the staff lounge I talked incessantly - nothing strange about that - and felt that I was on cloud nine.

This was a moment of history which would transform the whole life of BINC. I recalled the years of financial struggle, the early years which had been for some of us challenging but difficult.

How I wished that Dr Ford had lived long enough to join with me in acclaiming the success of the staff, for whom this was a time of fulfilment. I began to reflect on the years of endeavour and vision. I recalled the fact that Dr George Sharpe had insisted back in 1946 that students should have Scottish university entrance requirements before entering college. Many saw that as a pipe dream. Then the choice of college motto, "Scholarship on Fire". Many were certain that there was little scholarship and some wondered if there was any fire. George Frame had expected that both would come and that together both would be held in tension.

When I had returned to Hurlet in 1952 as a member of staff I wanted above all else to see the academic standards raised to the place where we could offer our young people the very best in Christian education. Members of the Board of Governors had always encouraged us to go for the best. It was this maxim which made them invite Dr Alex Deasley and Dr Jack Ford to join the teaching staff and when we were looking for new property in 1958 one of the main criteria was that we should locate close to a university with which we might affiliate. This was one reason why Manchester was such a prime area for our search. Professor F. F. Bruce, who was such a friend to us, was then the John Rylands Professor of Biblical Criticism at Manchester. The ideal was always to go as far as we could to give the best teaching possible.

Since that afternoon in Winnipeg I have given much thought to the process and the people who made this accomplishment possible. The first real step was taken when Canadian Nazarene College granted BINC affiliation. From the start we had insisted that any student graduating with the ThB must possess the entrance qualifications required by a British university. That was not a requirement made by CNC, but was self imposed in order to leave no doubt that the degree was in no way inferior to a British one. Scores of students will testify to the fact that they worked harder for their college degree than they did later when taking post-graduate degrees.

The college retained, at the centre of its aims, the preparation for ordination which had been central to its founding. We sought to avoid conflict between the spiritual and the academic and always insisted that they were two parts of one goal. Indeed, to develop spiritual maturity, one must be prepared to be stretched as fully as possible intellectually. It was with this in mind that we had tried to build a staff of competent scholars who were at the same time committed churchmen.

Dr Harvey Blaney began to lay the foundation of a curriculum which would demand the best results from each student. In 1976 he was followed as Academic Dean by Dr T. A. Noble. Dr Noble developed the programme so successfully that we began to think in terms of a British degree. How to start on this programme was the question.

The pattern set by London Bible College looked a likely road along which we might go, and, encouraged by the high standards achieved by our students, the staff, led by the Dean, began to promote the idea amongst the degree students of spending a further year at college after the completion of their ThB. to prepare for the London external degree of Bachelor of Divinity.

This would be the first time that our teaching staff would have their work examined by an outside body of scholars. To appreciate what we were undertaking it must be understood that our students would be competing in examinations with students who were in residence at the University of London and who were being taught by the lecturers who would set the final papers. BINC, of course, had no input into either the content of the curriculum or the final assessment of the students.

The plan was put into effect and in 1982 our first two candidates, Donald Maciver and Lee Boon Chong, successfully sat the examinations and graduated with the London University Bachelor of Divinity degree. Since Lee was a blind student this success was even more noteworthy. At his graduation Lee was presented to Princess Anne, the Princess Royal, who was Chancellor of the University. This was truly a red letter day for the college and each of us involved in their course work was greatly encouraged.

This first success was to be followed by others, and not one student presented for the London degree failed. In fact, two of our students who sat the first part of the degree examinations took first and second place in the entire country. For several years this seemed the direction which we would take; however, there was another option open.

In 1964 the British government had established the Council for National Academic Awards (CNAA), a national body charged with validating all higher education outside the university sector. It was mainly concerned with the polytechnics, but other private colleges had been able to come under their umbrella. Two of the first to be thus validated were London Bible College and St. John's College, Nottingham. Both had followed the London BD route we were pursuing, but gaining recognition would not be easy.

We were given encouragement by our friends from London Bible College to pursue CNAA validation of our own degree. As early as 1977, in his Dean's report, Mr Noble stated that after a number of years of presenting candidates for the London BD, "we may apply to the Council for National Academic Awards (CNAA) for our own BA degree. This is not a short term prospect but it is a goal which we are already keeping in mind in our curriculum planning and development of library facilities." Such recognition would imply that we had a place amongst the leading Evangelical theological colleges in Britain.

A second matter of importance was our library holdings. While Dr Blaney was Dean we had refurbished the music room and were using it for the housing of the library. Our friends from Bolton Church of the Nazarene at Daubhill had built shelving for us and this had been a great help. However, the space for books and study was very limited. We thought about ways and means by which we might add a new library facility. A large property came on the market at the end of Lancaster Road. This building, St. Michael's, could be developed to provide needed married student housing and facilities for the library. We made an offer, but were outbid, and it was purchased for development as a nursing home.

It was at this time that the owner of the property adjacent to the college, Dene House, was granted planning permission to develop the grounds as a housing estate. I was talking to this neighbour, Major Raffles, about the development and asked him what was to happen to Dene House itself. He observed that it would be sold: the asking price was to be £150,000, but, he suggested, it might be available to old friends for £140,000. That was £30,000 more than we had offered for St. Michael's, but Dene House was an attractive proposition.

The location of Dene House meant that we could expand our central campus by joining both properties. I began to do some calculations, but it seemed the required figure was more than we could hope to find. We still had a small mortgage on the married student housing in Clothorn Road, had only recently made the final payments on the chapel and dining hall, and had stretched the generosity of our church constituency to its limit. But we did need another building for a library, and this opportunity might never come again once the property was sold. We managed to get a Swiss loan through the good offices of European Nazarene College and so, in 1986, Dene House became the property of British Isles Nazarene College. Financially, it was a massive undertaking, which was not made easier when at the next District Assembly budgets were frozen. I am writing this almost seven years after the purchase of Dene House and the debt remains crippling. Nevertheless, there is little doubt that this move was an essential ingredient in the college's subsequent developments.

Tom Noble had now served as Academic Dean for eleven years. His own academic programme had been halted on several occasions. He needed a change from the pressure in order to complete his doctoral thesis and get to some other writing. In 1987, Dr Kent Brower, who had been at Canadian Nazarene College for eight years, accepted the invitation of the Board of Governors to return to BINC as Academic Dean.

Kent arrived in 1988 and brought new energy to the task. Tom Noble had taken over from Harvey Blaney and over the twelve years since had laid a solid foundation. More than that, he had begun building a strong superstructure of academic excellence which now enabled Kent, his colleague and friend, to develop the curriculum in such a way that systematic plans were implemented to achieve full accreditation under the auspices of the Council for National Academic Awards.

If this dream was to become reality then BINC needed to develop a higher profile among Evangelicals in the Manchester area and beyond. Prior to Kent Brower's return to Canada in 1979, he and Tom Noble had mooted the idea of an annual series of public lectures which would be distinguished by their high calibre. The staff was very positive about this, and the first of these lectures was given by the late Professor F. F. Bruce. He had been a friend to the college for many years, having supervised the studies of Dr Deasley and Dr Brower. This provided an excellent point of genesis for what were to become known internationally as the "Didsbury Lectures," lectures which have now become part of the theological calendar in Britain. The annual publication of these lectures has also raised the college's visibility. A succession of well-known British scholars (Marshall, Torrance, Atkinson, Barrett, Walls, Skevington Wood, Guthrie, Hooker, Clements, Dunn, Gunton and Clines) and two professors from Nazarene Theological Seminary, (Deasley and Bassett) have followed Bruce in this distinguished series.

We had good staff and were demonstrating that the teaching of the college was of the highest calibre, but consideration had to be given to other matters. In order to offer a viable honours theology degree course, specialists in major disciplines were essential. In 1977, the college had a developing staff of increasingly high academic quality. When Dr Brower received his PhD in 1978, the staff had its first PhD since the retirement of Dr Jack Ford. Mr Noble was poised to begin his research, and Bill Rolland was considering further postgraduate study.

But those days were not to last. Mr Rolland left the college at the end of 1978 and Dr Brower resigned to take up a post at Canadian Nazarene College in 1979. A few years later Norma Downie resigned to move to Edinburgh and Herbert McGonigle was elected District Superintendent of the South District of the Church of the Nazarene. In a small institution such as ours, these were major losses. Much time and energy had to be spent coping with this loss, a loss made worse by budgetary restrictions and the fact that there were still too few qualified women or men to fill the gaps. Several crucial appointments were made at this time: Revd Christopher Cope in Pastoral and Social Theology, Revd Tom Haverley, who was pursuing PhD research at Edinburgh, to teach New Testament from 1980 to 1982 and Mrs Heather Bell as part-time librarian. Other short term and part-time appointments were made, and visiting lecturers enabled us to function, but this was unsatisfactory if we were to achieve our goal.

It seemed that the dream would remain just that unless staffing problems could be resolved. The quality of the instruction was still of a high order but the impermanence of the situation made serious application to the CNAA unwise. Years would pass before the staffing strength was such that we could give serious thought to the whole question of accreditation. It was, however, to come sooner than even the most optimistic would have thought.

In 1985, it was evident that Mr Noble would need some kind of sabbatical leave if he was to complete his doctorate. Dr Brower, with whom we had kept in close touch, had a sabbatical leave due from Canadian Nazarene College and he readily agreed to assume the role of Acting Dean. This was the first time in six years that the academic staff had been at full strength, and we felt that we should begin to take some action. Dr Donald Guthrie, who had been instrumental in the negotiations which led to CNAA recognition for London Bible College, came to give the Didsbury Lectures. He agreed to meet with the staff to talk about the possibilities of getting CNAA recognition. He suggested that we should approach Dr Peter Cotterell, also of LBC and long term member of the CNAA Theological Studies Board, for more formal, but still unofficial, advice.

Dr Cotterell visited the college on 13th November 1985, made a thorough investigation of all aspects of the college's resources and then wrote an assessment. The four areas highlighted in this report were as follows:

1. The need to acquire and develop Dene House. The Board of Governors had already agreed to purchase this property which was adjacent to The White House. This, in Cotterell's view, would allow us to develop an acceptable suite of buildings. The fact is that without that purchase CNAA accreditation would have remained a pipe-dream.

2. The need to bring the library holdings up to date.

3. The need to prepare for external scrutiny. This would require Dean and staff to formulate and articulate policy and coherent academic programmes.

4. The continued need to strengthen academic staff who would need to be ready for continual self appraisal.

The question which we now had to ask was simply, "Can we meet these goals?"

Dr Brower observed in his 1986 Dean's report that "a long term vision for BINC has been of the day when we could offer our own British-validated degree. That day may now be closer than we thought." That report marked a turning point in the history of the college, for, in response to it, the Board of Governors voted unanimously to begin the process of seeking a relationship with the CNAA.

The road was not to be easy, and the destination seemed far distant. Dr Brower, invited to stay as Dean, felt that he should remain at CNC. In addition, staffing changes multiplied: I had reached retirement, and Mr McGonigle was elected Principal; Revd David McCulloch came on staff as a specialist in Pastoral and Social Theology; the college had to depend on visiting lecturers in some of its main areas of instruction; Mr Noble returned to his post as Dean, but had still to complete his PhD studies. This meant that the matter of CNAA was placed on the back burner. We desperately needed more permanent academic staffing arrangements.

In 1987, Dr Brower was again invited to return as Dean, and the Principal set as a goal full associate relationship with CNAA by 1990. For financial reasons the offer to Dr Brower was withdrawn, but was renewed in 1988. Dr Brower accepted and arrived in August of that year. Gordon Thomas was added to the teaching staff as instructor in Biblical Studies. Peter Rae, who had been Dean of Students from 1984, resigned to accept an appointment as Dean of Men at CNC, and Gordon Thomas assumed the role of Dean of Students. Gordon had completed an MA degree at London Bible College; Mr Noble was close to completing his Edinburgh PhD; Mr Cope was making progress on his Manchester MPhil and Mr McCulloch had plans to embark on a PhD at Glasgow. In addition, Mr McGonigle was about to begin a new PhD programme at Keele.

The stage was set for growth, and 1989 was a crucial time in the life of BINC. The dedicated, painstaking work of Mr Noble had established a strong foundation, so when Dr Brower came to build the final structure the task was made easier. In short, the meticulous work of the previous decade made the rapid progress to full accreditation possible.

Only those who were engaged in the endless committee meetings, spurred on by the indefatigable energy of Dean Brower, can truly testify to the mammoth accomplishment of those months. Visits to other colleges and endless discussions of programmes led to a 16-page presentation to the CNAA, and to a consultative visit to CNAA offices in London. Dr Brower writes:

Operating under the unanimous mandate from the Board of Governors in 1986 and confirmed in 1989, and after exhaustive and careful preparation, on 7th November 1989 the staff, administration and students of the college submitted the docu-

mentation necessary for recognition of the college as an Associate Institution of the Council for Academic Awards ...

The whole process involved a complete metamorphosis of the college... Nothing symbolised the change more graphically than the fact that the college changed its name from British Isles Nazarene College to Nazarene Theological College, effective 1st September 1990.[30]

The validating body was high in its commendation of the submission paper prepared by Dr Brower. Both validation committees were unanimous in their approval and encouraged the college to proceed to make application for a Master's programme, which was approved by the end of 1991.

Hardly had the staff caught its breath after CNAA accreditation had been secured when the government published its White Paper on Higher Education which proclaimed the demise of the CNAA. Were we to lose so soon what had taken so long to achieve? Negotiations were started with several universities and on 27th July, 1992, documents were signed on behalf of the University of Manchester by the Pro-Vice Chancellor and, on 31st July, 1992, on behalf of the college by the Principal. This formalised an associate relationship with the University of Manchester. Thirty four years after the move of the college from Glasgow to Manchester the dream of affiliation became a reality, and saw the college treated as an academic institution of university status.

Dr Brower, commenting on the whole procedure, wrote:

Thus, the vision for the college possessed by Dr Rae came to fruition. And if anyone were to have told the members of the staff and the Board of Governors in 1985-86 when this whole process began that this college would end up as a respected affiliate institution of a world class university like the University of Manchester, it would have seemed like an impossible dream. Many persons had a part in this journey.[31]

The writer is compelled to add that without the total dedication of all the staff and the expertise of Dr Brower in drafting an acceptable academic proposal the opportunity might never have been seized. Timing and enthusiasm were combined to bring all to fruition so that the dreams of the founder and succeeding leaders were finally realised. God surely brought together a team of men and women to make the final outcome so worthwhile. A year later, at the suggestion of CNAA officers, the college presented, and had approved, a one-year post-graduate MA course in "Aspects of Christian Holiness". I shall say more about the staff over the whole fifty years of the college in the next chapter.

The detailed information for this chapter has been gleaned from a paper prepared by Dr Brower. It seems proper and helpful for me to include this paper in its entirety in Appendix 1 for interested readers.

Photo No 45
Staff Members in 1989

Photo No 46
Students, Staff and Visiting Preachers at Fortieth Anniversary

Chapter 13

DEVELOPING A TEAM

The heart of the college, across the years, has not been the facilities, however fine they may have become. Indeed, it is not the college's affiliation and accreditation, however much we have striven for these things. The heart of the college has been the team of women and men who, through the years, have transmitted to and modelled for their students the twin goals of intellectual rigour and spiritual devotion: "Scholarship on Fire!" They have been the map makers who have shown their students the way ahead.

While recognising the academic limitations of the early staff, it is essential to recall the wealth of experience and the level of commitment to the cause of Holiness ministry which these men and women brought to the college.

We may not have learned all about contemporary Biblical Studies from teachers like Revd J. D. Lewis and Revd David Anderson, but the daily impact of the Bible on their lives and their understanding of the Bible in terms of its life application was profound. One graduate recalls: "In Revd David Anderson, I met one of the deepest spiritual preachers and Christ-like characters I have ever known." [32] David Anderson had been one of the three students to attend Dr Sharpe's college in Motherwell in 1926,[33] and his influence on his subsequent students spoke eloquently of the godliness of his character. J. D. Lewis was another saintly preacher whose eloquence was proverbial and whose intimate knowledge of the Bible and prayer life were influences which I would not have wanted to miss.

Revd James Macleod, BSc, every inch a radical believer, possessed a pattern of life and a sacrificial spirit which, together with his intellectual ability, made him a profound influence in theological matters. He would often be diverted by one or another student into Practical - rather than Systematic -Theology. His anecdotes from Greenock (where he pastored for several decades) were all introduced to the class, and a rather amusing incident comes to mind as I write. He and his family lived a very spartan life while they were in Greenock. His pocket watch did not boast a gold chain, but was adorned with a pleated shoe lace. His lectures were always held on a Tuesday morning and after the lecture we had a chapel service. On the occasion in question a special preacher was visiting the college. We had already met him, though Mr Macleod had not, and we had noted that all his teeth were filled with gold fillings. We managed, during the class period, to ask Jim what he felt about people who had gold fillings, instead of more ordinary fillings. To our astonishment he answered that since gold would last longer than other fillings it was probably the best stewardship. Later in the morning when the preacher walked in, I can still remember the look of triumph in the eyes of Jim Macleod, who saw immediately the little trap we had prepared in our question!

Dr Arthur Fawcett taught classes in Literature and History in the first years that the college was operating. His incisive and captivating style consistently challenged us to be better students. He had begun teaching the History of English Literature in the October term of 1945. I joined the student body in the April term of 1946 and, since I was studying for London University Matriculation by correspondence, asked to sit in on his classes. How stimulating they were! The fact that I passed with good grades was due in large part to the many hours that I spent with the splendid lecture notes provided by Fawcett. It was a great loss when he was unable to continue teaching. It would be impossible to forget the lectures in Homiletics given by Dr George Sharpe. His own mastery of the art was well recognised and his careful assessment of the student's outline gave us a good foundation. He was then in his 82nd year. He was followed by Revd William Robertson, who still lives in my memory for his oft-uttered phrase, "Boys, jot this down."

Revd Sydney Martin began to lecture in Church History in the Autumn of 1947. He had previously travelled to college from Twechar to attend classes and was a successful student in all subjects. He returned to the classroom immediately on graduating and taught Church History from October 1947 until we left Hurlet in 1958. His enthusiasm and encouragement spanned the decades, as he sat year after year as a vital member of the Board of Governors.

Other early "sessional lecturers" included two university graduates who came to teach once each week. Miss Jean Cameron (now Mrs Whiteford) taught English Literature and Miss Margaret Taylor, whose brother William Taylor had been a pastor, came to teach German to a small group of the students.

Other pastors who taught in the 1950s included Revd David J. Tarrant, then pastor at Port Glasgow. His preparation for class was always of a high order and his commitment to the work of the college positive. The two Henson brothers, William and John, different in style but, sincere in their search for truth and understanding, were often called upon to teach courses during those early days in Hurlet.

The Revd Stanley Tranter taught the Doctrine of Holiness. His classes were never left in any doubt about his commitment to the doctrine of Entire Sanctification. His loving spirit, revealed to us as a family in days of trauma, will always stand out as a demonstration of a man whose heart was filled with compassion for his fellows.

Two resident teachers were Mary Mellinger, who taught English, and held her degree from Eastern Nazarene College, and Olive Bangs who taught Greek and Biblical studies and who was a graduate of Pasadena College and Nazarene Theological Seminary. Margaret K. Latta MBE, many years a missionary to Swaziland (where she founded schools and the Nazarene Teacher Training College), came each week to teach English, and also served on the college Board of Governors. Music classes were taken by Mrs Sylvia Pollock, a pianist and music teacher from Paisley.

This was the team of men and women who carried us through some difficult times and places. Their spiritual impact was such that we had a longing to be more like them.

After we moved to Manchester we continued to depend on pastors coming each week to teach. These included Revd Dr Thomas Schofield, Revd Dr T. C. Mitchell, Dr Grant, Revd Melvin W. Quick, Revd Brian L. Farmer, Revd Leslie Evans, Revd Raymond Spence, Revd Dr Albert J. Lown, and others.

There is no doubt about the debt which we owe to all of those who gave years of service with little if any reward. I would have no history to write if these dedicated men and women had not given of themselves, their time, and their talents.

As the college grew, however, it became evident that the excellence required to develop successful church leaders demanded an exceptional academic programme, something that could not be achieved without expert and full-time staff. It was to the development of such a team that we gave ourselves in the decade of the seventies. In 1973, when I returned as Principal, the foundations had already been established. Dr T. C. Mitchell and Revd William Rolland had served under Dr Ford, and to this team were added men like Dr Harvey J. S. Blaney and Kent Brower. This was as yet a staff in the making, still dependent on visiting lecturers. Whatever our aspirations in 1973, it was to be a number of years before a full resident staff of able scholars would be in place.

In 1978 Bill Rolland decided to take a leave of absence, which eventually led him in new directions. The next year Dr Kent Brower felt led to return to Canadian Nazarene College to teach. In different ways the going of these two men was the most serious loss since the resignation in 1969 of Dr Alex Deasley. It was evident that the Board of Governors must give serious consideration to the financing of the college if a strong, permanent staff was to be built.

While it was still essential for us to use part-time lecturers, we needed to have men and women with specialised ability in their field. Tom Noble worked towards this goal during the decade from 1976 until my retirement in 1986. His success in building an exceptional team is affirmed by the fact that during this period all those students who sat the London University External Bachelor of Divinity degree were successful: a tribute both to Dr Noble and to the company of full-time and part-time staff which he secured.

Students from these years will remember such visiting lecturers as Revd J. Y. Muckle, retired Old Testament scholar, who had spent many years as a staff member at Hartley Victoria Methodist College. He taught Hebrew until his sudden death in 1980. Then, providentially, Mervyn Richardson, from the Near Eastern department at the University of Manchester, undertook to teach Hebrew. Other visiting lecturers in these years included Anne Jackson (N.T. Greek), Geoff Austin (Communications), Richard Griffiths (speech); Chris Bristow (New Testament); Barry Bryant and Dwight Swanson (Old Testament); Lois Rolland, Colin Wood, Dorothy Ardern, Kieron McNiff, Crawford Howie, Helen Richardson and John Haines (Music).

Part-time lecturers came on several occasions. Some were on sabbatical leave; Reuben and Mary Jo Welch from Point Loma Nazarene College, and Alex Deasley from Nazarene Theological Seminary. Andrew Downie and Nunzio and Monika Faranda had taken the London BD and were a great asset as instructors in these difficult years. Retired elders such as Sydney Martin, Jack Ford, Albert Lown in addition to Len McNeil (then pastoring in Ashton-under Lyne) came to teach in the summer terms.

The constant change in the 1980s meant that the small core of permanent staff was carrying a heavy teaching and administrative load. In 1980 the permanent staff consisted of Norma Wilson (Librarian), Tom Noble (Academic Dean), and Herbert McGonigle (Senior Tutor). Revd Chris Cope was then invited to join the staff. Chris, like Norma, was a graduate of the college. He had completed his BA at Manchester University and, during the 1980s, pursued his MPhil there. Chris had been a visiting lecturer at BINC whilst he taught and pastored in and near Atherton, and his addition to the college staff meant a considerable strengthening of the full-time staff. Like others, he wore several hats, and one of the tasks which fell to his lot was the editing of the *BINC LINK*. These colleges graduands brought with them a depth of understanding of student issues which was a key in the development of new college structures.

Other full-time staff members were part of the college scene in the mid- 1980s. Anita Blackburn was a Glasgow graduate who taught Church History before going to teach in Africa, where her career was cut short by her untimely death. Kenneth MacRitchie, grandson of Revd Kenneth McRitchie (an early pioneer pastor), was with us for a year teaching Old Testament. Revd Leslie Evans came as chaplain and lecturer in Pastoral studies and Homiletics, while Peter Rae served as Dean of Students and lecturer in English.

Other areas of college life were being strengthened, as various administrative responsibilities were transferred from the Principal to an Administrative Assistant. Len Taylor, a graduate of the college, was initially appointed to this post. On his departure Phyllis Reed assumed office responsibility until, in 1980, Eleanor Brocklebank, a graduate who had served as a missionary nurse in Papua New Guinea, took the post. During her seven years on staff the administrative operations of the college were systematically restructured, and finances carefully husbanded. Secretarial help, too, has been worthy of note. Lois Rolland was the first of a long line of office workers, a list which must include such stalwarts as Karen Ehrlin, Norma Wilson, Lynn Batt, Marcelle Trotman, Jean Prestwich, and Rita Stuart. Interesting stories could be told about the faithful and committed service of each of these and others. Suffice it to say that the record of their service will not be forgotten in the minds and hearts of students and colleagues.

Over five decades of college life the catering corps has been both diligent and long-suffering. In the early years, ladies from our local churches helped us for very small remuneration; Susan Irvine, Nurse Townsend, and Mrs Frizzell are names with which early students are familiar. Grace McIntyre from Ardrossan, followed by Maureen Reaney, were the first resident cooks in the 1950s. With the uniting of Beech Lawn and Hurlet, May Kneebone became matron in charge of catering. Others who followed her footsteps were Lily Tuckley, Michael Armitage, Joe Reid, and Geraldine Roberts. Since 1979, the names have included Jane Pavey; Maureen & Clay McLean; Dorothy Langler; Linda White, Gina Nicholas and, currently, Bridget Willkie.

From 1952 until 1966 Nan Rae was in charge of the planning and purchasing of groceries and housekeeping items. With a restricted budget, frugality was imperative, but despite economies we were, on the whole, able to maintain a good balanced diet. Students may beg to differ, with recollections of those days when they feasted on pigeon pie from the fertile back lawns of the college! In recent years, however, the Principal has not had to resort to the double-barrelled shotgun to provide fare for the dining hall tables, and instances of prayer and fasting have been occasioned by spiritual rather than financial exigencies.

As previously indicated, in August, 1986, Revd Herbert McGonigle was elected by the Board of Governors as Principal. His association with the college as student and staff member had spanned almost three decades. His love of the college was demonstrated in many ways over those years, and his election was well received by the constituency. He assumed the responsibility of planning for institutional development, and it seemed, despite the continued financial anxiety brought about by the purchase and financing of Dene House, that staff development could proceed.

This equilibrium was shattered by a proposal from the 1987 British Isles South District Assembly finance committee; it would, at a stroke, reduce the college budget by some £3000 at a time when the anticipated increase (£2000) would have enabled the college to take care of the repayments on Dene House. The eventual compromise, which froze the budget at the 1986 level, made the financial struggle still arduous.

With this development, staff additions would be more difficult, but they were nonetheless essential. Revd David McCulloch was invited to join the staff as lecturer in Practics. This area would need special care, and was one which would form an important element in the new degree structure.

In 1988 a number of events came together which resulted in staff additions. Peter Rae, who had been Dean of Students for the previous four years, left the college to give time to his own academic development. With his resignation, Gordon Thomas assumed the work of Dean of Students, which he combined with lecturing in English and Biblical studies. Another event of extreme importance in 1988 was the return as Academic Dean of Dr Kent Brower. This made it possible for Tom Noble to pursue his own academic work and to complete his thesis, which earned him his PhD from the University of Edinburgh. Thus by September there were seven members of faculty (including Heather Bell, a graduate and now a fully qualified librarian). Here, at last, was the nucleus of a teaching team which enabled the new Academic Dean, Dr Brower, to forward the affiliation process.

Herbert McGonigle and Tom Noble had gathered a core of first-class teachers together and when Kent Brower returned in 1988 as Dean the dream of twenty years before, of an academically strong team had at last been realised. Gordon Thomas had completed his MA at London Bible College, Chris Cope his MPhil at Manchester, Tom Noble his PhD at Edinburgh. David McCulloch and Herbert McGonigle were both working towards their PhD degrees at Glasgow and Keele respectively. It was no wonder that the Pro-Vice Chancellor of Manchester University referred to Nazarene Theological College as "a prestigious theological college in south Manchester."

During these past eight years, under the leadership of Dr McGonigle, the college has reached a position of strength which does credit to that leadership and to the committed ability of the entire staff. It should be remembered that, although a recognised Wesley scholar for years, his committed churchmanship and full-time load had prevented the completion of a doctorate he more than deserved. It is therefore the more gratifying that he should have completed his PhD at Keele University with such distinction. As a result of his work he is undoubtedly now one of the leading authorities on John

Wesley. He is also noted for the valuable collection of Wesleyan artefacts which he has gathered over the years.

In addition to the full-time staff, the continued valuable teaching of Anne Jackson and the addition of Dr Sylvia Osgood contributed greatly to the robustness of the college programmes. In recent years part-time lecturers have included Dr Paul Bassett from Nazarene Theological Seminary and Dr Sam Powell from Point Loma (both on sabbatical), Gerald Berglund (brother-in-law of Dr Eric Jorden) and Revd Don Maciver. Heather Bell and her assistant Barbara Bramwell continue to improve the library services.

With the resignation of Eleanor Brocklebank in 1987, Carolyn White, a recent graduate, took over responsibility for office administration: David McCulloch became Bursar and Chris Cope, Registrar. These administrative positions are the key to the smooth operation of the college at management level. The current Bursar, Denise Whittle, carries heavy responsibility, and is ably assisted by Rita Stuart, secretary to the Academic Dean and Registrar.

When, in 1984, John Edgar was invited to come as Maintenance Supervisor a step was taken which brought a dedicated Christian tradesman to us. His skills have not only kept the fabric of the building in good repair but have also added to the facilities of the college and saved literally thousands of pounds for the institution. Others, like Pauline Clegg, the housekeeper, keep the mundane daily details of college life in order.

The coming together of the present team has clearly been providential and, as a people, we must thank God for the commitment and dedication of these women and men who have left more lucrative careers to find a calling and vocation in service to God and the church, a calling which brings challenge and meaning. 1994 is the Golden Jubilee of the college: what better time to recognise all those who have, through devotion and skill, brought the college to this hour. Young men have indeed seen visions, and those visions have been brought to fulfilment. This is not only a tribute to past colleagues: we would affirm and salute those who, with ability and integrity, serve this present age. We believe in them and love them for who and what they are. They are colleagues: past and present; professor to housekeeper. It has been an honour and privilege to share in the realising of a vision, and words do scant justice to my sense of privilege at having been part of this group of women and men.

Yet behind the team of staff are ranged countless other teams of men and women who have built this vision, who have served on the Board of Governors, or have supported the college in the constituency. Over the past fifty years men and women from all walks of life have served as members of the Board of Governors. On them has fallen the responsibility of giving overall direction to the college. Their vision in the first decade was decisive in helping to establish a basis on which future members could build. In the second decade it was this board which was faced with the challenge of relocation, of the disposition and acquisition of properties.

It was the members of this board who laid plans to build Hurlet Hall, Beech Wing, and the Maclagan Chapel and Dining Hall; who had the vision to approve the purchase of Dene House and the other off-campus properties. This board has always offered encouragement and support, not least in their acceptance of responsibility for the raising of finances. The fact that the college property is now valued at more than one and a half million pounds is a miracle of providence; it also suggests that those board members made astute decisions through the years, and used wisely the £8,500 realised from the sale of Hurlet and Beech Lawn. I must note, too, our debt to the General Church. Over the years the Board of General Superintendents, the NYPS, the Department of World Missions, and the General Church of the Nazarene has, through financial support and vision, ratified its sense of responsibility to the church world-wide.

Dr Edward Mann, Executive Secretary of the Department of Education, gave us personal and practical support and his influence encouraged us in the building of the J.B.Maclagan Chapel and the new dining room. It has been a privilege to have General Superintendents visit with us on the college campus. Dr George Coulter was the General Superintendent in jurisdiction when I returned to the college in 1973. He was also the first to speak at a college graduation. Dr Eugene Stowe officially dedicated Dene House as the new Library. The late Dr Charles Strickland was in jurisdiction for five years and during that time gave us his ear and his support on numerous occasions.

Finally, it is important to put on record the debt of gratitude the college owes to its supporters, those British Nazarenes who, through their budget payments, their planned giving through gifts and legacies, and their own personal sacrifices and labours, affirmed their faith in the work of the college. God has certainly honoured the faith of all those early pioneers, whose vision makes the celebration of this Golden Jubilee possible.

Chapter 14

LIFE DOES NOT STAND STILL

The history of any college is the story of men and women interacting at the level of teacher and student. It is also the story of changes in the society around us and the manner in which these changes affect the lives of all engaged in the pursuit of learning. Elsewhere in this story I have hinted at the fact that changes are essential in the method not only of the teachers but in the life of the community. It is something of that development that I wish to record in this chapter as it not only forms part of the general summary of the fifty years but is also an important matter in the present life of Nazarene Theological College.

In the first decade there was, as I have said, little opportunity to set out a philosophy of education or administration. The main function in that decade was to try to ensure that graduates were able to cover the required course for ordination. The home study course was followed with little variation and in consequence learning was more by rote than research. This was the inevitable pattern since most of those who taught were themselves products of the home study course. This was to be followed, with few exceptions, until the early sixties.

In a questionnaire sent out to former students over the fifty years the following question was asked: "In what ways did the college fulfil or fail to meet your expectations?" A graduate of 1950 wrote, *This question is rather unfair to the college at that time, since the curriculum was limited, and the teachers were untrained. I was by nature a scholar, and usually read far beyond the teaching. The college prospectus promised introduction to academic subjects which it could not fulfil. Surprisingly, there were no tutorials for more able students.* The same graduate noted other aspects of college life when he wrote:

"When writing of Hurlet College, in the early days, one must not be too critical. A few years after the Second World War, food rationing was still in operation. The college was allowed one egg per person per week. (Sometimes it arrived rotten, and that meant that a student did not get an egg that week.) I can remember that the Golden Syrup used on the morning porridge had to cease, because of reported college stringencies. Even the porridge had to stop, when milk ran short, because Blossom the cow was ill. Large tins of jam were sent from America. After they were opened they were always locked away in the kitchen cupboard between meals. Over a period, many sacks of small hard beans were boiled up in a large pot for students who were arriving back to college on Sunday evening. Many were the agonies endured through the night watches!"[34]

In the first two decades there was little provision made for students who were married. At the end of the war when some older students came this was not seen as a major problem. Some of us moved into residence and our wives remained at home with children, if there were any, and found work.

The discipline of the college was according to a strict timetable. Students would be awakened by 6.30am. By 7.30 am each would be attending to domestic duties which were regularly assigned. Classes would begin at 9.00am and each class would be two hours in length. Lunch was served at 1.00 pm and after dishes were cleared away all students would be out on manual labour for two and a half hours each afternoon. Tea was served at 5.00 pm and from 6.30 to 9.00 pm all would gather in one room for evening study. A handbell was rung announcing each of these events. Prayers and devotions were held daily and prayer and fasting was a regular feature. Each Tuesday we met for chapel service.

The study hour was not a particularly easy way to prepare and tended to be less fruitful than private study would have been.

The reason for this method would have as much to do with the problem of heating as with the felt need to keep students under supervision, although I am sure that the latter played a part. Lights were due to be out by 10.30 pm (a practice not strictly followed in the early years). The required rising time was 6.30 but students could opt to rise earlier. Some rose by 4.00 am and wrapped themselves up in warm clothes and a heavy dressing-gown in order to get extra study in. Bedrooms had no central heating. Sometimes students would sneak in an electric fire and use that from time to time. It was strictly forbidden but (as I recall) freezing feet tended to affect the ethical considerations. One hopes that absolution has been given to those "bounders" who dared.

I am sure that there were many frustrations with the regimentation but we still had considerable freedom. Permission could be obtained to be out after lights-out if necessary.

This was the pattern of life, with some variation, through the first twenty years. Of course these were the days before the permissive society brought its influence to bear on all areas of young life. It was relatively easy to see that students were in on time when all were housed in the one building. It was even suggested that the Principal had a periscope which he pushed up the chimney stack to see any late comers. I really wish I had thought of that!

The move to Manchester and the building of the student residences made the oversight of students a little more difficult. When we were planning to build Hurlet Hall and Beech Wing it was decided that a master switch be installed in the main administration building. Students I am sure will recall that if lights were still burning after 11.00 pm I threw the switch, putting the students in darkness. The switch was put on again but if ten minutes later still saw lights on then the master switch would put the residences in darkness for the rest of the night.

Looking back to those days one wonders at the seeming necessity for such rules. It took some experience of life in another culture for me to realise that trust and respect for adult young people might well achieve more than rigid rules. Two graduates writing about their years in college reflect on the impression left with them. Revd Dr William Stewart, now district Superintendent of the Canadian Atlantic District of the Church of the Nazarene says:

The basis of my philosophy of ministry were laid during my college years. While I could make a general statement and say the teachers of the college helped me form my approach to ministry, I must personalise it and mention some names in particular. Revd. David Tarrant taught me Pastoral Theology and Homiletics. He was himself a successful pastor and taught me how being a pastor can be one of the most exciting, stimulating and interesting jobs in the world. I have always believed that, and since then, true enough, although I have experienced many problems in the ministry, boredom and lack of excitement have not been amongst them. Dr Sydney Martin taught me Church History but the real lesson of his classes were gracious godliness and holy wisdom. I aspired to be like him but never attained it. Dr Hugh Rae, while he taught me many subjects, he also taught me many lessons. Discipline and hard work; loyalty and faithfulness; consistency and integrity were qualities of leadership I saw in him and tried to incorporate into my own ministry style." [35]

Grace Burrows, missionary in Switzerland, writes:

My years in BINC "opened windows" in my mind academically and spiritually. I thoroughly enjoyed my time there and, if circumstances had permitted, would have loved to have stayed longer.[36]

In the first years life was not as frustrating as this account may suggest. The comradeship between staff and students was on the whole very fulfilling. I write of course as one who was at the administrative side most of the time and perhaps it would be valuable to hear some other points of view on this matter. Revd John Paton, now a District Superintendent writes,

Highlights began my first day at college when I realised how little I knew of Christian terminology. Hearing each male student addressed as "Brother" I imagined I was the odd man out having a recognisable first name. Yet I always felt I truly belonged. I was in the place that God wanted me to be... The first time we fasted and prayed for three days I felt that not only was I in a life changing experience but the college and the church were going through a similar experience.

He continues, on the fun side of it,

Ian Hall blowing up the Aga cooker in the kitchen, Jim Martin being held fast against the wall by Dr Deasley's dog Dago and Philip Bedwell looking with despair at his beloved bush hat dangling from the weather cock...I was glad we were taught and shall ever be grateful for the examples - to always give of our very best and not to seek out any reward save the satisfaction of serving Christ and the Church.[37]

It was inevitable that changes would come over the years. Sometimes students were frustrated by the "unnecessary" disciplines. Rules and regulations somehow seemed like they were cast in iron. The changes in leadership did not appear to bring much change until the late 1960s, then students began to ask why such rules were required. It is amazing how when called upon to give a rationale for such requirements the answer seems difficult if not impossible to find.

It was this dilemma, among other factors, which led to the preparing in 1974 of "Guiding Principles for College Life". Here was a determined effort to move the emphasis away from rules to be accepted and obeyed, towards establishing a basis on which to build one's own philosophy of life. This, it was hoped, would give students the impetus towards higher living because the importance of knowing what one wanted would act as a stimulus.

Guiding Principles for College Life

British Isles Nazarene College, then known as Hurlet Nazarene College, was established in 1944 as the educational institution of the Church of the Nazarene in Britain. In 1959 the college moved to its present location in Manchester.

Through these thirty years of its history the prime purpose of the college has been that of serving the Church. Men and women entering her ministry have for the main part come by way of the college. The spirit of the college campus is an important factor in influencing the and in this connection we each - staff and students - have an important role to play. The spiritual dimensions of the college can only be measured by the spiritual commitment of each life and to this end it is our prayer that we each enter upon an ever closer walk with God. Our commitment to God is our most vital asset as individuals and as a community.

This is an educational institution and in consequence we must maintain a high standard. Careless application of the mind and in the use of time cannot produce the results essential to a growing person with a desire to serve God and the Kingdom. To this end - the development of the whole person - the college must strive.

The Individual
a. It is essential to spiritual growth that we each seek to feed our soul in the private meditation of God's Word. There is no substitute for this.

b. To maintain a spirit of love to those around us is important. If personal hurts are allowed to grow they will destroy any possibility of growth in Christ. It is essential to keep the channels of communication open.

c. In a community like ours we depend upon each other to a very large degree. Hygiene is a basic necessity for us all. Tidy rooms and surroundings make life much more pleasant. Remember the old adage, "It is easier to keep this place tidy than to make it tidy". Tidy habits are so often a reflection of a tidy mind which is so much more useful in God's service.

Community.

a. The disciplines required are not designed to be points of dispute, or contention but give due regard to the development of personal discipline and community relationship.

b. The college programme is designed for people who are seriously concerned about learning which will fit them for life. The rules of the college have such people in mind. The frivolous mood of the holiday camp is not of value in the college. So late night and such habits are seen as a deterrent to our real purpose.

c. Mature adults need to use time and opportunity wisely. We therefore expect that study hours will be used with purpose and that we will remember that those around us have the right to quietness and consideration. Courtesy at all times is an essential Christian grace.

d. Classes are arranged to give each student the maximum time in which to develop mentally, spiritually and physically. Attendance at class is expected unless hindered by sickness or matters entirely beyond you control.

e. Leadership requires men and women with commitment and initiative: neither of these alone will suffice. We believe that you are here because of your commitment and thus have evidenced some initiative. The staff and the student council will do all they can to plan opportunities for service. In the long run, real effective ministry will depend on you as an individual. Involvement is a personal thing. Whatever planning is done to develop field service, each has the obligation to find an avenue of regular commitment.

<u>*Achievement*</u>

The setting of standards and goals is an important element in human life, and we should make these in a realistic and determined manner. Always ask more of yourself than you ask of others. It is as easy to be an optimist as a pessimist, and more rewarding. God needs optimistic realists, to understand that this is His world, that He is in control. We do well to remember this in the days of discouragement and frustration. The temptation to set your goals too low, or to doubt the validity of God's call on your life will be very real. Remember when He calls he also enables us to equip ourselves. Set the highest goals of preparation for yourself and then relax in the Lord about their realisation. Study - to show thyself approved of God...

This document marked a distinct attempt to move from the regimentation of individual lives to the placing of responsibility where it rightly belongs, namely, in the hands of each individual. It is never an easy road along which to travel. The temptation to lay down rigid rules of discipline is a tantalising temptation to the administrator but experience has shown that it must be resisted if the best results are to be achieved. It is a self-confident student body which is now being served by the college and one in which the academic demands make discipline an essential for success. Each generation of students has played a major role in the life of Nazarene Theological College and this book salutes them as men and women of high integrity and serious endeavour.

EPILOGUE

It has been my intention to recall some of the high moments in the growth and development of Nazarene Theological College. Forty years have passed since I was invited to join the staff of the college. From the first days of my involvement I have tried to be concerned with the lives of those who were seeking to prepare for ministry in some area of the church.

In the first years of George Frame's leadership and in the first period of my own service up until my resignation in 1965, most of what we wanted to do remained little more than a dream. There were, of course, steps taken from time to time which brought the dream closer, but so often it seemed that other matters crowded out the ideal towards which we struggled.

If little seems to have been said about students, it is not because they have been of little importance. Indeed, they have been at the very heart of our existence. Changes may have at times seemed to be in the interests of the institution rather than of the individual, but those of us who have been students know the difficulty of suffering through rites of passage which will benefit only a later generation.

Over the past months, as I have been recalling the life of the college my thoughts have been drawn to students. What a wealth of ability and resources they represent! I cannot think of them without a sense of wonder at how they touched my life and the lives of my family. Indeed, as I write this final chapter my heart swells with emotion and my eyes fill with tears: not of sorrow, but of great joy in the wealth and richness that have been mine through years of contact with the finest and most dedicated group of people which it has been my privilege to serve.

Memories come flooding back of students whose lives have been dedicated to the service of the church. They are to be found serving God around the world, graduates who say with pride, "I was at Hurlet...at Beech Lawn...at The White House, Didsbury."

Not all who came found the fulfilment they sought and this must always be a source of regret. I am sometimes haunted by the thought that we might have done something differently to have given them a more firm foundation, particularly in those early years, when the quality of college life was ever changing. Yet it was those of you who were students, both you who seemed to succeed and you who appeared to fail, who have composed the kaleidoscope of our lives. To serve you was always our aim, and to have you serve the Lord, sometimes in unpredicted ways, will always be our joy. We have looked at those early struggles for survival and at the frustrations which students had to combat in the years that are gone. However, the triumphs to which this history bears witness are far beyond those early dreams, and place the doubtless points of failure in their proper perspective.

There are, of course, those who talk about the "good old days" with a sense of nostalgia, even voicing a hope that those days might return. Yet the passing of some elements of college life must in truth be seen as a blessing. The memories which we cherish are not always faithful to the facts. Who would choose to exchange the warm study-bedrooms of today for the cold, crowded rooms of Hurlet? Who would want to exchange the quiet comfort of Dene House with its excellent library facility for three antique Hurlet bookcases and their motley collection of old, uncatalogued and often redundant books? I for one have more than enough memories of what the old days lacked to shed too many tears for the past! Like parents who look at their independent and mature adult children, and briefly wish they were still babes in arms, we reflect on the early days of college with a nostalgia that does not wish to cling to the years of adolescence!

We now need, at this half-century mark of the college, to look to a future which calls us to grasp with both hands the opportunities it offers. This college has left some of its early struggles behind. It does not now need to justify its place in the life of the church. It does not need to feel less than proud of its academic distinction, formed by the efforts of so many men and women over these fifty years. What its present Board of Governors, its faculty and staff, and its supporting constituency do need to ask are some questions about its future place in the life of the church in Britain, and, more particularly, in the life of the Church of the Nazarene.

Central to our purpose must be the development of men and women who are deeply committed to the mission and message of the church of God. Nor must we forget our allegiance to the denomination to which we owe our origin and from which we draw our basic support, and its emphasis upon that commitment to God which allows the Holy Spirit free access in directing and motivating each individual. I, with others, have consistently held that there is no essential dichotomy between the spiritual and the academic. That position I have held for many years and have never been tempted to change. This understanding is formed by the fact that in my own student days the spiritual was all too often deemed the only matter of importance, so the academic could be brushed aside if it interfered with so-called spiritual activities. The truth is that only as men and women seek for the best in their intellectual pursuits can they truly become spiritual giants. In offering less than our best in all areas of life we are saying that God, who has given us ability and the opportunity, should be satisfied with less than our best.

Some will misunderstand this and in their search for knowledge lose the vitality of their faith. That does not mean that faith and learning are incompatible, but suggests rather a failure to maintain the balance and tension which are part of faith. May future generations witness that we are endeavouring to keep Christ centre stage and are at the same time bringing all our talents to God that they might be multiplied in blessing by Him.

I recall an illustration from the life of one who was a great influence on the college, namely the late Professor F. F. Bruce. Professor Bruce was a regular member in a small Christian Brethren fellowship. Into that fellowship came a man who had lived a life of sin and, as a older man, had found Jesus Christ as his Saviour. In the work place, those who had known him in his unregenerate days would ask all kinds of questions about the Bible which he could rarely answer, but he would always say at those times that he would find the answer. On Monday mornings when he returned to his work mates he would bring some very pertinent responses to their questions. When asked where he found his answers he replied: "There is an old fellow at our church called Fred who seems to know all about these things." What a trenchant lesson that is! He knew nothing of the fame of Professor Bruce, but knew a great deal about the Christian humility of a deeply spiritual brother who seemed to have the answers.

We must hold in tension the faith once delivered while investigating all the sources at our disposal to discover more about the God to whom we are committed. This is a rare challenge, and one which we would grasp with both hands believing as we do that our faith can walk hand in hand with our search for truth. We must always remember that not all that is stated to be truth is, in fact, truth. We must remember always that Jesus is, for the believer, "the Truth". Many so-called truths must be held lightly until the day of Christ's appearing, when all shall be revealed. We must not diminish the worth of the search yet must hold fast to our commitment of faith. If we are "saved by grace through faith" then we must not seek for any more secure foundation even though we explore all that comes to be explored. It was the late Dr H. Orton Wiley who remarked, "Ignorance has no part with holiness."

High on this decade's agenda must be the development of a system of support which will enable the college to continue its central role in the life of the church. This is and must remain our college: that it should serve a wider field in the Christian community is an end towards which we have been moving over the past years. The growth of the student body is an essential part of the ministry of the Church of the Nazarene here in Britain. It has never been our policy to confine ourselves to those of our own denomination, and a growth in the number of non-Nazarenes at the college will mean that the church and its doctrine has gained a voice and a hearing in the Christian community. The fear that this will somehow change the commitment of the college to the mission and message of the church is unfounded; whoever comes will find that the ethos of the college and its central message are not only theoretical but that *in practice* we seek to demonstrate the Christian ideal of perfect love.

A larger student body does, of course, serve to make the college more financially viable, but that should not become, by default, the financial lifeline of the institution. There is a need for Nazarenes whom the Lord has prospered to make their contribution to the stability of the college, perhaps by establishing and developing a Capital Fund or Foundation from which the college can draw interest over the years. An initial fund of £500,000 is a realistic goal for such an institution as ours, and would encourage further such endowments. This "Year of Jubilee" would be a fitting time to initiate such a capital investment. Funded from legacies, corporate donations, and individual generosity, it would feed its interest into future college development, and remain in perpetuity, allowing the college the basic resources to fulfil its mandate and extend the influence of college and church.

This mandate, however, cannot be fulfilled without the continued desire of our young people to serve God. This urgent desire is what has brought young people to college over the years, and pastors and people must keep before their youth the privilege of being called of God to serve Him. As this century comes to a close we begin a new century in which the changes of the past will be surpassed by greater change in the future. The mission and message of the church will be challenged in new ways, so let us re-affirm our commitment to Christian Education and the outreach of the church which comes from that.

The story of Nazarene Theological College has only begun. These have been years in which God has shown that His hand is upon the ministry of the college. As we move into the next half century of service let us pledge our support wholeheartedly. Whoever writes the college's centennial history, if Jesus tarries, will be recording for that generation the faithfulness of those who have had vision and commitment to the future. May the fire of the Spirit continue to burn in all our hearts, and may intellectual endeavour bring an enlightenment which will serve to fuel the flame of the Holy Spirit in each of us. May "Scholarship on Fire" always characterise the influence of the college and of all whose lives are touched by it.

Photo No 47
Students and Staff 1993

Appendix 1

The Quest for British Degree Validation
Kent E Brower

When Dr Rae returned from Canada in 1973 to assume the Principalship of the college, he brought with him some of the lessons he had learned during his five years in Canadian Nazarene College. One of the most important ideas was the conviction that BINC could offer degree-level education. His arrival, along with the arrival of Dr Harvey J. S. Blaney, the retired New Testament scholar, former head of the Department of Religion and sometime Academic Dean of Eastern Nazarene College, set in motion a chain of events which would eventually bear fruit in 1990 four years after Dr Rae's retirement.

Canadian Nazarene College had already been validating a course in South Africa leading to its BSL degree. Before he left, Dr Rae had negotiated an agreement with CNC to validate a course at BINC leading to the Bachelor of Theology degree. Introduction of this course was revolutionary. Until then, the college had been a rather traditional British Bible college. Now, with this new course, the college introduced methods of teaching and assessment which would only become common in British higher education two decades later.

Dr Blaney, a Canadian by birth who had long experience of the North American system of modular courses, credit hours, semesters grade point averages and other rather strange terms to British education, was the ideal person to implement the new programme at BINC. He was to give two years of extremely valuable service before he returned to the USA and Mr T A Noble assumed the role of Academic Dean.

In order to sustain the breadth required in the ThB curriculum, the college had to increase its staff strength. Curriculum itself was modified to come into line with the Canadian degree, which was in turn designed primarily to meet or exceed the ordination requirement for ministry in the Church of the Nazarene. This meant that the academically more able students could now work to degree standard while completing their theological education. Instruction at the college was now quite consciously pitched at degree standard, a policy which enhanced the educational experience of all students, whether or not they were degree candidates. The first degree students were graduated from the college in 1976.

British higher education in the form of the new polytechnics was already beginning a process of revolution itself which would ultimately affect the "old" universities as well. But it would be fifteen years before British universities would make access to degree-level education less elitist. In this climate, the college deliberately insisted that entrants to the degree course should fulfil the normal degree entrance requirements for any British university, rather than the more lenient standards allowed in Canada. Thus, only a minority of students at any one time were on the degree course. This insistence upon entrance qualifications ensured that students on the degree course already had demonstrable ability to perform at the same level as their fellow students in the universities.

Mr Noble's arrival as Academic Dean proved to be another important step forward. He brought to the college a thorough education in theology, experience in a secondary school classroom, and a commitment to excellence as well as a considerable awareness of the British higher education scene. Also important for the development of the college was the fact that he had been the very influential secretary of the Evans Commission on the Ministry and the College. Soon after the report was published in 1976, Mr Noble was the Dean of the college and in a position to superintend the implementation of the Commission's recommendations in the college and to encourage adherence to its terms by some others less committed to quality education for ministry. That report became the framework for ministerial education in the Church of the Nazarene in the British Isles and has been influential in most of the subsequent developments in British Nazarene ministerial education. The ThB formed the cornerstone of the whole British Nazarene theological education edifice.

The introduction of the ThB was not seen as the final development at BINC, however. Because the degree was validated in Canada, its recognition in Britain outside Nazarene circles was very limited and strictly *ad hoc*. Some graduates were able to pursue post-graduate qualifications. Indeed, one of the first three graduates, after obtaining a PGCE and having several years of teaching experience, went on to complete a postgraduate course in the University of Manchester. But there was no general recognition of the degree and this lack was a serious limitation to any who were interested in postgraduate study in Britain.

To meet the needs of students who were capable of completing postgraduate study in theology, the staff decided to prepare some students simultaneously for the external Bachelor of Divinity (BD) granted by the University of London. This degree was a widely recognised, British-validated qualification, acceptable in all contexts.

The college was delighted when its first BD candidates graduated in 1982 with excellent degrees. Mr Noble commented that 1982 was for the college "the breaking of the academic sound barrier." Although subsequent developments would relativize that achievement, it was significant if for no other reason than that it confirmed that the standard of education being offered at the college not only met the requirements of Canadian

Nazarene College but also were at a level comparable with that at other British institutions of higher education.

From the college's point of view, however, the London BD had serious drawbacks. First, the college had no input into either the content of the curriculum or the assessment of the students. Although there was some overlap between the strictly academic theology of the BD and the wider curriculum of the ThB there was a number of areas which did not correspond. The BD was more narrowly focused on what might be called "academic theology." The needs of the church and the students at the college were better served by the wider curriculum of the ThB which included a significant component of "practical theology."

Second, the method of assessment, being restricted entirely to written final examination papers, was very traditional and, most agreed, paedagogically unsatisfactory. The university set the syllabi and the examinations for this course; everything else was left to the student. In short, although the end result was a recognised British degree, the approach to degree work could only be considered satisfactory if no other option were available.

Happily, such an option was already available in principle. In 1964, the British government of the day established the Council for Academic Awards (CNAA), a national body charged with validating all higher education outside the university sector. Its primary concern was the new polytechnic colleges which were initially established to deliver technical and vocational education in parallel with the universities and at a comparable standard to that which applied in the Universities. This new body could also validate courses in private institutions. Amongst the first private Christian institutions to seek validation of their awards from the CNAA were London Bible College and St. John's College, Nottingham. Both institutions had strong academic records. Both had offered tuition leading to the University of London BD. But even with these credentials, gaining recognition from the CNAA was not an easy task. Neither of them succeeded at the first application. But the possibility was there and LBC eventually became the first Evangelical college in Britain to receive this recognition.

The tantalising prospect of similar recognition was already a point of informal discussion by the staff of the college. As early as March 1977, in his Dean's report, Mr Noble stated that after a number of years presenting candidates for the London BD, "we may apply to the Council for National Academic (CNAA) for our own BA degree. This is not a short term prospect but it is a goal which we are already keeping in mind in our curriculum planning and development of library facilities."

Recognition by the CNAA would imply that the college had a place amongst leading Evangelical theological colleges in Britain. But outside denominational circles, the college was virtually unknown. Even in Manchester, few in the wider church and academic community know anything about it. The college needed to establish a place in these circles. With that thought in mind an annual series of public lectures of a high academic standard was first mooted. Acceptance of this idea was readily given by the staff and the first annual series of Didsbury Lectures was delivered in 1979 by Professor F F Bruce, Professor Emeritus and former Rylands Professor in the University of Manchester. Professor Bruce who had been the academic advisor of Dr Deasley and Dr Brower, gave these lectures a solid beginning on which to build the outstanding series which now is part of the theological calendar in Britain. Publication of the majority of these lectures also gave the college visibility in the academic sphere far beyond its campus. Scholars who are household names in theological circles, Marshall, Torrance, Atkinson, Barrett, Guthrie, Hooker,

Clements, Dunn, Gunton, to name some, have all followed Bruce in this distinguished series. The college was now on the map.

The academic staff of an institution is its most important asset. In order to offer a viable honours theology degree course, the college needed specialists in the major disciplines. In 1977, the college had a developing staff of increasingly high academic quality. When Dr Brower received his PhD in 1978, the staff had its first PhD since the retirement of Dr Ford. Mr Noble was poised to begin his research and Revd Bill Rolland was considering further post-graduate study. But those days were not to last. Mr Rolland left the college at the end of 1978 and Dr Brower resigned to take up a post at Canadian Nazarene college in 1979. A few years later, Norma Downie resigned to move to Edinburgh and Revd Herbert McGonigle was elected as District Superintendent of the South District.

In a larger institution, the effects of such losses would have been minimal; in a small institution, the effect is inevitably greater. Dr Rae and Mr Noble spent much of their energy in coping with this problem often hampered by the budgetary restraints and the lack of qualified British Nazarenes. Several crucial appointments were made in this period including Revd Chris Cope in Pastoral and Social Theology and Mrs H M Bell as part-time Librarian. Other short-term or Part-Time appointments were made and the services of several Visiting Lecturers enabled the college to function but a stable institution needed permanent staff. The goal of CNAA validation was still there and developments in library and curriculum were still taking place. But no other concrete steps could be taken. The dream was still only a dream. Indeed, it could be nothing else until the staffing problems of the college could be solved. It would be some years before the full complement of permanent academic staff could be reassembled in a satisfactory fashion.

In 1985, Mr Noble received a sabbatical leave to complete his doctorate. Dr Brower, himself on sabbatical leave from Canadian Nazarene College, assumed the role of Acting Dean. That year the academic staff was once again at a full complement; it was time, therefore to take some action.

During the 1985 Didsbury Lectures, the staff took the opportunity of raising the matter of CNAA validation with Dr Donald Guthrie, who had himself been instrumental in the negotiations which led to CNAA recognition for London Bible College. He suggested that the college approach Dr Peter Cotterell, also of LBC and a long term member of the CNAA Theological Studies Board, for more formal, but still unofficial, advice.

Dr Cotterell visited the college on 13th November, 1985, made a thorough investigation of all aspects of the college's resources and then wrote an assessment for the college. Cotterell highlighted four areas which needed careful consideration:

1. The acquisition and wise use of Dene House. The college had already agreed to purchase the property adjacent to The White House. In Cotterell's view this purchase could enable the college to move from its then current "barely adequate" facility to a quite acceptable academic plant. In fact, without this purchase, the college was at its limit with no prospect of CNAA validation.

2. The identification of gaps in our library holding. Miss Judith Shiel, the theology specialist at the John Rylands University of Manchester Library, was invited to conduct a thorough inspection of our library to identify area for remedial purchases.

3. Preparation for external scrutiny. Such scrutiny would require a considerable expenditure of time by the Dean and staff to formulate and articulate policy and coherent academic programmes.

4. Addition of quality staff members. While the situation looked promising during the 1985/86 academic year, staff strength would have to be maintained. Members of the academic staff would need to be more diligent about self-development as academics and professionals.

All of this was expected, of course. But the remarkable thing was that all these areas of concern could be addressed within the capacities of the college. As Dr Brower observed in his 1986 Dean's report, "A long-term vision for BINC has been of the day when we could offer our own British-validated degree. That day may now be closer than we thought." That Dean's report marked a significant milestone in the direction of the college, for in response to the report, the Board of Governors voted unanimously to begin the process of seeking a relationship with CNAA.

There was to be a further delay in the process, however. Although Dr Brower was invited to remain as Dean, he felt obliged to return to Canada, partly due to staffing problems at CNC. This, combined with the retirement of Dr Rae in 1986, left a gap in the staff. Mr McGonigle, who had already returned as a full-time member of staff, was elected Principal of the college and Revd D. McCulloch was added to the staff as a specialist in Pastoral and Social Theology. But for the next two years, the college had to revert to covering most of the biblical subjects with visiting lecturers. Mr Noble returned to his post as Dean but it was essential that he continue to devote a considerable amount of his energies to completing his own PhD. He could not devote time to the preparation of the college for external scrutiny even if all other ingredients were already in place. They were not. It was clear that a more permanent solution to academic staffing would have to be found before any approach to CNAA could hope to be successful.

Although Dr Brower was unable to accept an offer to remain on staff in 1986, the college did invite him to return in 1987. That same year, the Principal set as a goal full associate relationship with CNAA by 1990. A few weeks after the offer was accepted, however, the Principal felt obliged to withdraw it for financial reason. The offer was renewed in 1988 and Dr Brower was able to assume the post in September 1988. At the same time Mr Gordon Thomas was added to the full-time staff in Biblical Studies, just after the completion of a CNAA MA degree at London Bible College. Mr Noble was close to completion of his Edinburgh PhD, Mr Cope was making progress on his Manchester MPhil, and Mr McCulloch had plans to embark on a PhD programme at Glasgow. Mr McGonigle was about to begin a new PhD at Keele after his time limit had expired at Leeds. The full compliment of qualified staff was finally in place.

Future historians of the British Church of the Nazarene may well point to 1989/90 as being one of the most crucial in the development of British Isles Nazarene College. The period from January 1989 to January 1990 was to be one of intense activity at the college. By the time of his January 1989 report to the Board, Dr Brower could report that action was now underway to reach the goal. Faculty had formed a joint staff/student CNAA Development Committee to spearhead the work. Over the next few months, endless committee meetings would be required to produce the documentations necessary to support the application to the CNAA. Curriculum revision proceeded through several stages, first within disciplines and then between disciplines. Policy was developed and adapted from appropriate models at other institutions. Constitutional revisions to provide the appropriate legislative framework for the emerging institution were drafted by Mr Noble and approved by Faculty before submission to the Board of Governors and ultimate ratification by the two District Assemblies. Dr Brower visited two theological colleges already associated with CNAA to discuss their experiences with the CNAA and gain further insight into the process of gaining recognition by the CNAA. Then, a consultative visit to the CNAA offices in London, conducted on the basis of a 16 page document submitted to them, led to the establishment of a tentative timetable which involved submitting a rough preliminary draft of our submission on 31st July with a first draft on 31st October and a final draft on 31st January 1990.

The actual course of events went somewhat differently. The rough draft arrived in London in early August after which Ms H Eggins, a CNAA official, paid a visit to the college and made many valuable suggestions for changes in our submission. A modified version was then submitted and discussed with CNAA officials in early October. At this meeting, the CNAA officials requested an accelerated timetable, with the final submission to be in London by 31st October. This meant that October was a very busy month with final decisions being taken on a number of details.

Operating under the unanimous mandate from the Board of Governors in 1986 and confirmed in 1989, and after exhaustive and careful preparation, on 7th November, 1989 the staff, administration and students of the college submitted the documentation necessary for recognition of the college as an Associate Institution of the Council of National Academic Awards. In the event, the material was there in plenty of time for the visit of the Inspection Team but the inspection visits were delayed until after Christmas.

Validation and approval of the college and its courses involved visits from two separate CNAA parties. The first visit determined whether the college was a suitable institution in which to offer CNAA awards.

After their Institutional Validation visit on January 10th, 1990 the visiting party made an unqualified recommendations that the college become an Associated Institution of the CNAA. On February 7, 1990 the Course Validation Visit approved the college's three and four year BA degrees. The first intake of students to the new courses occurred in September 1990 with retroactive enrolment for those students admitted to the ThB course in September 1989.

The whole process involved a complete metamorphosis of the college. Students were now active participants at all levels of institutional governance including the Board of Governors. External examiners were now required to scrutinise the work of the college.

But nothing symbolised the change more graphically than the fact that the college changed its name from British Isles Nazarene college to Nazarene Theological College, effective 1st September, 1990. Still, as the Dean remarked to the Governors in 1989, the changes were those which would be appropriate even if the college did not receive CNAA recognition.

At the same time, the Dean noted that this step was but the final one in a lengthy journey in the pursuit of quality education for our ministers. In fact, time was to prove that other steps were yet to be taken. As a result of the visits by the CNAA validation teams, the horizons of the college were set even higher.

The heart of the submission to the CNAA was a British-validated BA degree to replace the Canadian-validated ThB. But the validating team strongly encouraged the college to proceed immediately with a proposal for a taught MA course. Although somewhat exhausted from its arduous effort to submit documentation for the bachelor's degrees, during the next few months the staff worked to produce a three-track taught Master of Arts degree, including one track devoted to Christian Holiness. The proposals were submitted to the CNAA in time for a validation visit in December, 1990.

On this occasion the validating team made some significant suggestions for alterations to the proposed course. They judged that our resources would only allow us to support one MA course, a course to be called "MA in Aspects of Christian Holiness." The college was ideally placed to offer this course, one which would be unique in the UK and could be taken by two methods including distance learning. The course was approved for the first intake in September, 1991.

Recognition of the college by the CNAA brought with it the right to act as a Sponsoring Institution for supervising the Council's research degrees (Master of Philosophy and Doctor of Philosophy). This recognition brought the college to a state of maturity. All the ingredients were in place to ensure that the college could become a significant partner in Nazarene higher education as well as a contributor to the wider Evangelical cause in Britain. The Dean had been even so bold as to anticipate the next few years would be a period of refinement and improvement.

In May 1991, however, the government published its White paper on Higher Education. Much in that paper was welcomed by all in higher education. What was not welcomed by colleges such as Nazarene Theological College was the announced demise of the CNAA.

Only two options were open to the college, namely, to seek an acceptable degree-validation arrangement with a recognised degree-granting institution or to forfeit all the advances made as a consequence of the CNAA relationship. The latter choice was unthinkable; the only realistic option was the first.

The CNAA offered two main attractions to the college. First, it dealt with the college entirely at arms length, thereby ensuring that the autonomy and mission of the college would not be compromised in any way.

Second, it was prepared to accept our modular delivery of the course and its deliberate integration of the practical and the academic recognition by the CNAA virtually guaranteed that the college could expect ready acceptance of its courses by a new validating body.

Informal preliminary discussions began with a number of universities with a view to new validation arrangements. As a consequence the Board of Governors approved the following resolution at its March, 1992 meeting:

> *The Board authorises the Academic Board to negotiate a suitable arrangement with a degree-awarding body in the UK to replace the current CNAA validation, provided that any new arrangement preserves the autonomy, ethos and mission of the college in the same measure as implied in the CNAA recognition.*

On that basis, the Academic Board made formal enquiries to three potential validators: the Open University, the University of Wales and the University of Manchester. After careful consideration of the options, the Academic Board determined to seek and affiliation relationship with the University of

Manchester. Although gaining affiliation with the University of Manchester would involve more preparation including new validation visits, such an affiliation promised to be the best option available to the college, satisfying our requirements on all points.

On 27th July, 1992, documents were signed on behalf of the University by the Deputy Vice-Chancellor and, on 31st July, 1992, on behalf of the college by the Principal formalising the affiliate relationship with the university. The relationship included validation of all the college's taught courses and approval of the research degree courses when appropriate regulations were in place at the college. That final stage in the agreement was formalised in 1st April, 1993. Included in this affiliation agreement was recognition of all members of the college's current full-time, part-time and visiting teaching staff. At its Graduation Day service on 10th October, 1992, the college graduated its first student who completed a University of Manchester degree at the college. It was a poignant day for all.

Thus, the vision for the college possessed by Dr Rae came to fruition. But it is unlikely that even someone as prescient as Dr Rae could have predicted this conclusion when he returned to Manchester in 1973. And if anyone were to have told the members of the staff and the Board of Governors in 1985-86 when this whole process began that this college would end up a respected affiliate institution of a world-class university like the University of Manchester, it would have seemed like an impossible dream. Many persons had part in this journey. When one reflects on the paths that have been taken, the way that the right people seem to have come together at the right time, the collective wisdom which was being exercised at all levels, is it too much to detect the purposes of God in it all?

Appendix 2

GOVERNORS

Men and Women who have served on the Board of Governors

The first Board of Governors were appointed at the British Isles District Assembly of the Church of the Nazarene, held at Parkhead in 1944. These were as follows:

Revd Dr George Frame; Revd Peter Clark; Revd Arthur Fawcett; Revd William Robertson; Revd David Anderson; Revd James B Maclagan; Revd John D Lewis: Mrs Emily Frame; Mr Charles Cullen;

From 1946 onwards Governors were elected to serve and the following all served varying periods and are in alphabetical order:

Revd Geoff Austin;	Mr William Barclay;	Mr Sam Boal;
Revd George Brown;	Revd Ray Busby;	Mr Sydney Cairns;
Mr Geoff Clarkson;	Mr Sam Cootes;	Mr Tom T Corser;
Revd John Crouch;	Mr Percy Davies;	Miss Rosemary Davidson
Mr Victor Edwards;	Revd Leslie Evans;	Revd Brian L Farmer;
Mr Donald Flint;	Mr F W Flitcroft;	Revd Dr Jack Ford;
Mrs Mary Garrick;	Revd Peter Gentry;	Mr Ian Gillies;
Mr James Gotobed;	Revd Percy Gutteridge;	Revd Leslie G Hands;
Revd William Henson;	Mr David Henson;	Miss Vera Hiddleston;
Revd Maynard G James;	Revd Dr Eric E Jorden	Miss Margaret K Latta;
Mr Stephen Leach;	Revd Dr Albert J Lown;	Revd William Lynwode;

Revd Dr Sydney Martin; Revd Philip McAlister; Mr Norman McCulloch; Revd Dr H McGonigle; Mr John Macdonald; Revd Don Maciver; Mr Lyle McMillan; Miss Anne McNaught; Revd Dr T C Mitchell; Mr Walter Neil; Mr Raymond Newton; Mr James Noble Snr; Dr T A Noble; Mr W A Noble; Revd Trevor Overton; Revd J R Packard; Revd John Paton; Mr Tom Pollock; Revd Dr Hugh Rae; Mr Robert Reaper; Revd Leslie Roberts; Mr W W Sheasby; Revd Dr T W Schofield Mr Brian Souter; Revd Raymond Spence; Revd D J Tarrant Dr Paul Tarrant; Mr H Tattersall; Revd David Thirkell; Mrs Jean Thirkell; Mrs Vernita Tink; Revd R F Tink; Revd Stanley Tranter; Mr L C Shepherd; Mr Paul Wallace; Mr Peter Warman; Dr Philip Weatherill; Mr George Williamson; Mr James Williamson; Mr H E Wood; Revd C H Wood.

With the granting of degree status the Academic Dean, the Bursar and the student President were added to the Board of Governors:

Dr Kent E Brower Revd David McCulloch; Mrs Denise Whittle; Mr Mark Breathwaite; Mr Gordon Payne; Miss Tricia Moutray.

Appendix 3

CITATION OF MERIT

At each General Assembly of the Church of the Nazarene, Nazarene Theological College has awarded the **Citation of Merit** to the following:

- **1972 Revd Dr George Frame**
- **1976 Revd Dr Jack Ford**
- **1980 Revd Dr Sydney Martin**
- **1985 Revd Dr A R G Deasley**
- **1989 Revd Dr Hugh Rae**
- **1993 Dr Kent E Brower**

REFERENCES

	Page
1 Jack Ford, *In the Steps of John Wesley,* Kansas City; N.P.H, 1968 p. 43	12
2 Ford, pp. 43 - 44.	13
3 Ford, pp.56-57	14
4 Ford, p. 66.	17
5 Minutes of College Board of Trustees p. 1-20	28
6 Ibid, p. 7.	28
7 Ibid, p. 7.	28
8 Ibid, p. 8.	36
9 Ibid, p. 10	38
10 Ibid, p. 11	40
11 Ibid, p. 11 and 12	40
12 Ibid, p. 12	41
13 Ibid, p. 13 and 14	42
14 Ibid, p. 17 to 19	45
15 Ibid, p. 20	45
16 Ibid, p. 29	54
17 Ford, p.159	62
18 *The Flame,* XII, No6 (1946), p.10	63
19 *The Flame, p.1*	64
20 *The Flame* , XIII, No 6, (1947) p.20	65
21 Ibid. p. 20	66
22 Ford, p.160	66
23 Extract from letter written by Revd Hugh Gorman to the author 20-3-93	71
24 Revd John Weatherill article from *The Flame*, XVII, No1,p. 25	71
25 Gorman *(see ref 23)*	74
26 Ford, p.140	90
27 Ford, p.116	91
28 Excerpt from a letter from Norma Downie, written 29th March, 1993	92
29 Extract from letter written by Revd J Paton on 14/4/93.	95
30 From paper prepared by Kent Brower, See Appendix 1	137
31 Ibid.	137
32 From a letter written by Revd Dr George D. Stewart.	140
33 *From a conversation which the writer and Dr T.A. Noble had with Dr Sharpe's daughter Mrs Isabel R. Edwards, on 26th May, 1993. The other two students were Murdoch Luke and John Watson.*	140
34 Letter from graduate, March 1993	153
35 Letter from Revd Dr William Stewart 17/3/93	155
36 Letter from Grace Burrows 16/3/93	155
37 Letter from Revd John Paton 13/4/93	156

Index of Photographs

Photo No 1
Revd Dr George Sharpe founder of Pentecostal Church of Scotland 9
Photo No 2
1 Westbourne Terrace, Kelvingrove, Glasgow 15
Photo No 3
Revd Dr George Frame, Founding Principal of
Hurlet Nazarene College, Barrhead, Glasgow 19
Photo No 4
West Hurlet House, Barrhead, Glasgow 23
Photo No 5
George and Emily Frame with son Cyril 25
Photo No 6
Students and Staff at front entrance of Hurlet in 1948 30
Photo No 7
Cottage and Garage 34
Photo No 8
Dr Ted Martin presenting cheque for $10,000 37
Photo No 9
Students and Staff at front entrance to Hurlet, 1948 46
Photo No 10
Professor Kenneth Grider and students
in the lecture room at Hurlet. 47
Photo No 11
Manual Work at Hurlet on a foggy afternoon,
Revd Peter Clark Supervising. 47
Photo No 12
Union with I.H.M. Leeds, 1952 48
Photo No 13
Staff and Students, Hurlet, 1957 48
Photo No 14
1957 Graduation in Paisley. Speaker: Revd D.W.Lambert 49

Photo No 15
Summer Evangelistic team
L.-R Alex Jones, John Crouch, Hugh Rae, Cyril Frame 49
Photo No 16
*Farewell Gathering with Paisley Church of the Nazarene Board,
April, 1958.* 50
Photo No 17
*Revd Maynard G. James, first Principal,
Beech Lawn Bible College.* 61
Photo No 18
Beech Lawn Bible College, Uppermill, 1947-49 68
Photo 19
Beech Lawn Bible College and Flat, Stalybridge 68
Photo No 20
*Students and Staff of Beech Lawn Bible College,
Mottram Road, Stalybridge* 69
Photo No 21
*C.H.C. Ministers and families,
Beech Lawn Bible College* 69
Photo No 22
The White House, Didsbury, Manchester 82
Photo No 23
First Class of Students in The White House, 1959 83
Photo No 24
*Dr G. B. Williamson, General Superintendent,
officially opening Hurlet Hall and Beech Wing, 1961* 85
Photo No 25
Hurlet Hall, 1961 86
Photo No 26
Chapel Service in College Library, 1962 88
Photo No 27
Student Body, 1963 89
Photo No 28
Students and Lecturers, 1966 89
Photo No 29
Revd Dr Jack Ford, Principal, 1966-73 94
Photo No 30
"The three wise men of BINC" 95

Index of Photographs 187

Photo No 31
Students and Staff, Autumn, 1966 97
Photo No 32
Students and Staff, 1972-73 100
Photo No 33
Trekking party, 1964
from L-R Robert Brown, Bill Rolland,
Jim Martin and Gwyn Downing 102
Photo No 34
Students and Staff, 1963 103
Photo No 35
Students on College Week-end with Revd John Weatherill 103
Photo No 36
Students and Staff, 1967-68 104
Photo No 37
Revd Dr Hugh Rae, Principal, 1954-66; 1973-86 104
Photo No 38
Students and Staff, 1974 112
Photo No 39
J.B. Maclagan Chapel 120
Photo No 40
New Dining Hall adjoining the Chapel 121
Photo No 41
Unveiling of Plaque by Mrs Jean B Maclagan,
Revd Dr David Maclagan and Revd Dr Hugh Rae 121
Photo No 42
Dr Edward Mann giving dedication address, 1978 122
Photo No 43
Revd Dr Herbert McGonigle, Principal, 1986 - 126
Photo No 44
Revd Dr Eugene Stowe and Revd Herbert McGonigle
at the dedication of New Library, 1987 126
Photo No 45
Staff Members in 1989 138
Photo No 46
Students, Staff and Visiting Preachers at Fortieth Anniversary 139
Photo No 47
Students and Staff 1993 166

NOTES